MORE
Tastes & Tales
From Texas
With Love

By

Peg Hein

Illustrated
By
Kathryn Cramer Lewis

Hein & Associates
Austin, Texas

Cover Design by Kathryn Cramer Lewis

Editor: Mary T. Ullrich

Contributing Editor: Richard Zelade

Consulting Editor: Pete Lewis

First Printing	10,000	October 1987
Revised and Reprinted	15,000	March 1988
Third Printing	10,000	May 1989
Fourth Printing	10,000	February 1990
Fifth Printing	8,000	September 1990
Sixth Printing	8,500	October 1991

ISBN: 0-9613881-1-0

Tastes & Tales

This second book about Texas cooking and Texas happenings began to take shape without conscious effort or planning. Many readers of the first book **Tastes & Tales From Texas . . . With Love** commented on how much they liked the combination of tales and recipes. Often they would send a favorite recipe or a bit of history about their area — and so a file began to grow. And this book began to take shape.

It is a book that fits the way Texans cook. Most Texas cooks lead extremely busy lives and so they want recipes for preparing meals that look good, taste marvelous and take very little time. Now and then they are ready to do some serious cooking and they look for the recipe that is a challenge. **MORE Tastes & Tales From Texas . . . With Love** was written with these criteria in mind.

Gathering recipes and talking with people from all over Texas has been a wonderful experience. With thanks to all who contributed recipes and to all who will be cooking with them from all of us who produced the book, we give you now

MORE Tastes & Tales From Texas . . . With Love,

Peg Hein

CONTENTS

Tastes & Tales

APPETIZERS

Texas Ranch Scene

The hospitality of San Antonio's Menger Hotel has been famous since before the Civil War. William Menger, who had operated a brewery since the 1840's, found more and more of his customers needed a place to sleep. Menger would wipe the long tables in the bar clean and convert them into makeshift beds. In 1859 he built a hotel adjacent to the Alamo. It quickly became a favorite of the military, and it is said that Teddy Roosevelt did most of his Rough Rider recruiting at the Menger Bar. Step up to the bar today and ask for what T.R. drank and you'll be served a Boiler-maker — a stein of beer and a shot of whiskey.

Texas Hot Jalapeño Cheese

If you don't have a Texas-shaped mold, now is the time to get one. It's not essential to the recipe, but it does give that special Texas touch. Spread any left-over cheese on tortilla chips and bake until bubbly.

Yield: 16-20 servings

½ pound mild Cheddar cheese
½ pound sharp Cheddar cheese
1 pound Velveeta cheese
1 pound hot bulk sausage
9 fresh jalapeños, seeded and finely chopped

Melt the 3 cheeses together in top of a double boiler. Brown the sausage in a large skillet, stirring frequently. Drain and add to cheese mixture. Add the chopped jalapeños and pour into a 1½-quart mold. Refrigerate for 2-3 hours. Unmold on a large cheese board and serve surrounded by crackers, bagel chips or corn chips.

Note: Use rubber gloves or be sure to wash hands carefully with soap after handling jalapeños or any hot chiles. Their oil can be irritating to eyes and skin.

La Villita—"the Little Village"—is San Antonio's oldest neighborhood. It was originally a Coahuiltecan Indian Village on the banks of the San Antonio River. The first Spanish huts were thrown up about 1722 for the families of Spanish soldiers, and 100 years later the site had become one of the city's most fashionable neighborhoods. In December 1835 the Mexicans surrendered San Antonio to the Texans at La Villita. German, Swiss, and French immigrants later added their special flavors. The area was restored before World War II, and La Villita is now a quaint, city-owned, historic area with museums, entertainment, arts and crafts, and other attractions.

Tortilla Crisps

These little crisps may be used with soups and salads or made into a wonderful appetizer when spread with a cheese topping and reheated.

Yield: 48 pieces

6 10-inch flour tortillas
½ cup melted butter or margarine
½ cup corn oil

Cut each tortilla into 8 pie-shaped pieces. Place in a medium mixing bowl. Combine butter or margarine and oil, pour over tortilla pieces and soak for 20-30 minutes. Place pieces on a cookie sheet and bake at 400° for 10-12 minutes.

Cheese Topping:

3 ounces shredded Cheddar cheese
3 tablespoons chopped ripe olives
¼ cup finely chopped green onion
½ cup mayonnaise

Combine ingredients, spread on Tortilla Crisps and bake at 400° for 3-4 minutes.

Appetizers

The first Mexican "restaurants" in Texas appeared in San Antonio in 1813 when the "Republican Army of the North,"aided by U.S. agents, captured the city. Enterprising local women set up al fresco cafes in San Antonio's plazas to serve fiery native specialties to the curious and hungry invaders. The Anglos were soon driven out, but the "Chili Queens," as they came to be known, kept on serving. They even survived the destruction of most of their stands during the Christmas Eve 1862 rioting of Confederate soldiers. Eventually the Chili Queens enjoyed nationwide fame, serving to the likes of William Jennings Bryan and O. Henry. The 1893 Chicago World's Fair had a "San Antonio Chili Stand." San Antonio health officials finally dethroned the Queens in 1937, citing unsanitary conditions.

Mexican Roll-Ups

Yield: 50-60 servings

1 cup commercial sour cream
8 ounces softened cream cheese
1 4-ounce can chopped green chiles, drained
1 4-ounce can chopped ripe olives
¼ cup chopped green olives
1 cup grated Cheddar cheese
¼ cup minced onion
1 teaspoon garlic salt
12 flour tortillas
Chopped jalapeño peppers to taste (optional)

Blend sour cream and cream cheese until smooth. Add remaining ingredients (except for tortillas) and mix well. If tortillas are not flexible enough to roll easily, wrap in foil and warm in a 350° oven for 5 minutes. Spread cheese mixture on tortillas, roll up and place seam side down in a glass dish. Chill for several hours until firm. Slice into ½-inch sections and serve.

Its location on the University of Texas campus overlooking the Austin skyline is a magnificent setting for the Lyndon B. Johnson Presidential Library. The extensive archives, a replica of the Oval Office and photographs of several other rooms present a picture of LBJ's years in the White House. Lavish gifts from foreign heads of state are displayed, as well as one of the limousines used while he was president. Photographs, movies, recordings, displays and memorabilia are documentation of the life of President Johnson and the Johnson family. The old family photographs, their history narrated by President Johnson and Lady Bird, give a warm and intimate glimpse of their lives before, during and after the presidential years.

Mrs. Lyndon B. Johnson's Cheese Wafers

The recipe for these tasty, tender tidbits came from Lady Bird Johnson.

Yield: 30 wafers

1 cup soft butter or margarine
2 cups flour
8 ounces grated sharp Cheddar cheese
1 teaspoon cayenne pepper
½ teaspoon salt
2 cups Rice Krispies

Cut butter or margarine into flour; add cheese and seasonings and fold in cereal. Use a teaspoon to drop small circles of dough on an ungreased cookie sheet; flatten with the spoon. Bake at 350° for about 15 minutes. Watch carefully for the last 2-3 minutes as they should be only slightly browned.

APPETIZERS

El Camino Real—the King's Highway—was the major thoroughfare from Saltillo, Mexico, to the first Spanish missions in East Texas and was often called "Trail of the Padres." Domingo Teran de los Rios, Spanish provisional governor of what was to become Texas, marked the trail in 1691. Only the river crossings were marked, leaving the overland path between the crossings mostly up to the traveler. It followed old Indian trails in many areas as it meandered from near Nacogdoches through San Antonio and crossed the Rio Grande near Eagle Pass.

Empanadas de Queso

These little turnovers of baked pastry with cheese are a handsome choice for a cocktail buffet.

Yield: 2 dozen

Pastry:
- 3 cups flour
- 1 teaspoon baking powder
- 2 tablespoons shortening
- 3 teaspoons sugar
- 1 teaspoon salt
- 1 cup milk
- 2 eggs, separated

Combine flour and baking powder and cut in shortening until mixture resembles small crumbs. Dissolve sugar and salt in milk and add egg yolks. Combine with flour mixture and knead until dough is blended. (Do not overwork dough or pastry will become tough.) Divide dough into walnut-size balls. Roll out on a floured surface or pastry cloth into circles 4-5 inches in diameter.

Filling:
- 1½ pounds grated Cacique, Mozzarella or Monterey Jack cheese
- 8-10 green onions including tops, finely chopped
- 24-30 black or ripe olives

Mix cheese and onions. Place 2-3 tablespoons mixture in center of each pastry circle. Add black olive (optional). Carefully fold pastry over filling and seal edges by crimping or making a double fold. Glaze top of pastry by brushing with beaten egg whites. Place filled empanadas on cookie sheets and bake for 15-20 minutes at 450°.

Hickory-Smoked Almonds

Wonderful for a party snack. Be sure to make enough because people can't stop eating them.

Yield: 1 pint

2 cups natural, whole almonds
4 tablespoons melted butter or margarine
2 teaspoons Old Hickory-Smoked Salt (Spice Islands)

Mix almonds and butter in a 9x13-inch baking pan. Sprinkle with 1 teaspoon Old Hickory-Smoked Salt and place in a 250° oven for 20 minutes. Stir and sprinkle with more salt and return to oven. Bake for another 45-50 minutes, and drain on paper towels. Sprinkle with remaining hickory salt while still hot.

Crispy Bacon Bites

Easy to do, and really good.

Yield: 8 servings

8 very thin bacon slices
16 square stone ground wheat crackers or rectangular saltine crackers

Cut each bacon slice in half. Wrap bacon around cracker. Place on a broiler pan or a rack set inside a rimmed cookie sheet. Bake at 300° until bacon is cooked, about 25 minutes. Parmesan cheese may be sprinkled on tops during last 15 minutes if desired. Cool briefly on rack to crisp bacon and serve warm.

APPETIZERS

For decades the masthead for the *Fort Worth Star-Telegram* has carried the slogan "Where the West Begins." And since its beginning, Fort Worth has been an "aw-shucks" cowtown, the proud home of the southwest's largest stockyards. Dallas, on the other hand, always aspired to more refined, Eastern ways. Geographically, at least, Fort Worth is where the West begins. To the east is the Grand Prairie with rich soil for farming, and to the west are the North Central Plains, rolling and treeless, and best suited for ranching.

Cowtown Screws and Nuts

This wonderful snack disappears quickly. Any left over may be stored in plastic bags, frozen and thawed as needed.

Yield: 4-5 quarts

Seasoning sauce:

1½ cups bacon drippings
1 cup melted butter or margarine
3 tablespoons Worcestershire sauce
2 tablespoons Tabasco
1 tablespoon garlic powder

Heat ingredients and mix thoroughly.

Cereal Mix:

1 box Cheerios
1 large bag pretzels
1 box Corn Chex
1 box Wheat Chex
1 box Rice Chex
1 small bag Fritos
4 cups nuts, any combination

Combine cereal mix in 2 large roasting pans. Pour seasoning sauce over top and mix well. Bake at 225° for 2-3 hours, stirring frequently. Let cool before storing in plastic bags or in airtight containers.

Curried Cheese and Chutney Spread

This got raves from everyone who tasted it. It is also very easy to make. Just be sure you have the chutney.

Yield: 8 servings

1 8-ounce package cream cheese
1 10-ounce cold pack sharp Cheddar cheese
2 teaspoons curry powder
2 tablespoons finely crushed wheat crackers
½ cup chutney (Major Grey's or Peach Chutney — see Index)

Soften both cheeses (the cold pack cheese comes in a tub or a crock) and combine. Mix in curry powder. Refrigerate until cheeses become firm. Shape into a log and roll in cracker crumbs. Spoon chutney on top and serve with crackers and apple slices.

Quick Black-Eyed Pea Dip

This is a wonderful dip that can be made in the microwave oven in just minutes.

Yield: 6-8 servings

1 15-ounce can black-eyed peas with jalapeños
1 teaspoon garlic powder
4-5 green onions, finely chopped
8 ounces cubed Velveeta cheese
½ cup butter or margarine

Drain peas and mash until smooth. Place in a 1-quart bowl or microwaveable dish and add remaining ingredients. Microwave on Roast or Medium High for about 4 minutes or until cheese is melted. Stir well and pour into a serving bowl. Serve with corn chips or crisp raw vegetables.

Texans have been cooking by the book since 1883, when the Ladies' Association of the First Presbyterian Church of Houston published *The Texas Cookbook*, proclaiming it "the first enterprise of its kind in our state." Although truly Texan—with recipes for smothered squirrels, broiled venison steaks and mustang grape wine— nary a recipe for chicken-fried steak could be found in it, nor anything with jalapeños.

Corn Pup Appetizers

These miniature Corn Dogs make tasty tidbits for a casual party.

Yield: 10 servings

1 cup all-purpose flour
⅔ cup cornmeal
1 tablespoon sugar
1½ teaspoons baking powder
1 teaspoon salt
2 tablespoons melted bacon drippings
1 egg, beaten
1-1½ cups buttermilk
½ teaspoon baking soda
1 pound hot dogs
Oil for frying

Combine first 5 ingredients in a medium bowl. Add bacon drippings and mix well. Combine egg, buttermilk and baking soda. Add to flour mixture and stir until smooth. Dry each hot dog carefully and cut into 6 pieces. Heat 3 inches of oil in a saucepan to 375°. Dip each piece of hot dog in batter to coat and fry in hot oil until golden, turning as necessary. Remove with a slotted spoon and drain on paper towels. Insert party picks and serve with Corn Pup Dip.

Corn Pup Dip:

½ cup mayonnaise
¼ cup sour cream
2 teaspoons Dijon-style mustard
1 teaspoon lemon juice
1 teaspoon chopped pickle relish

Combine all ingredients and mix well.

Seasoned Oyster Crackers

These wonderful snacks are simple to make and, if frozen, can be ready to thaw and use when needed.

Yield: 24 servings

2 large brown paper sacks
2 12-ounce packages Keebler Oyster Crackers
1 12-ounce bottle Orville Redenbacher's Popping Corn Oil
1 1-ounce package Hidden Valley Ranch Salad Dressing Mix
1 teaspoon dill weed

Place one paper sack inside the other. Empty both oyster cracker packages into paper sacks. Pour popping corn oil, salad dressing mix and dill weed over oyster crackers. Close sacks tightly and shake gently to mix. Place closed sacks on something that will absorb oil (more paper sacks or newspapers) and let set for 24 hours, turning occasionally.

Pita Crisps

These are tasty as an appetizer or for snacks.

Yield: 10-12 servings

4 large, flat pita breads
½ cup softened butter
½ teaspoon garlic salt
½ teaspoon onion salt
¼ teaspoon celery salt
Dill weed

Slice each pita bread in half crosswise and open flat. Mix butter and salts and spread on inside of pita slices. Sprinkle dill weed over top and bake on a cookie sheet at 400° for 8-10 minutes or until lightly browned and crisp.

Microwave Toasted Pecans

You can have toasted pecans ready to serve in less than 10 minutes by using your microwave.

Yield: 2 cups

2 cups pecan halves
2 tablespoons melted butter or margarine
1½ teaspoons seasoning salt

Combine pecans, butter and seasoning salt in a glass baking dish. Microwave on High for 1 minute. Stir pecans with a wooden spoon until they are thoroughly coated. Return to microwave and cook on High for another 4-5 minutes, stirring once or twice. Spread on paper towels to cool.

Note: To toast pecans in a regular oven, use the same ingredients, coat pecans with butter and seasoning salt, and arrange in a single layer in a large, flat pan. Bake at 275° for 50-60 minutes, stirring every 15 minutes.

Orange Spiced Pecans

These extraordinarily tasty treats are marvelous for munching.

Yield: 3 cups

¾ cup sugar
¼ teaspoon salt
1 teaspoon cinnamon
3 tablespoons Tang orange drink powder
6 tablespoons milk
1 teaspoon vanilla
3 cups pecan halves

Combine sugar, salt, cinnamon, Tang and milk in a small saucepan. Cook over medium heat to soft-ball stage (234°), stirring frequently. Remove from heat. Add vanilla and pecan halves. Stir until mixture is no longer glossy but has a slightly grainy look. Spread on wax paper, separating so that nuts do not stick together. Let set for 1 hour before serving or storing in an airtight container.

Tastes & Tales

BREADS AND BREAKFASTS

State Capitol, Austin

Angelina is the only county in Texas that is named for a woman. Angelina was a Hasinai Indian girl who was educated by the Franciscan Fathers who founded the Mission San Francisco de los Tejas on the Neches River in East Texas. She helped the Spanish re-establish their mission in 1716 and 1721, impressing them with the authority she now wielded in her village and tribe. Historians disagree on whether she was a saint or a domineering woman. The Angelina River and a national forest were also named in her honor.

Clarkie Brown's East Texas Hush Puppies

Lufkin in Angelina County hosts the Hush Puppy Olympics as part of its annual Forest Festival each May, and Clarkie Mae's team has been the winner twice. That's fishing country, and they know their hush puppies. Bet you, too, will judge these the best you've ever tasted.

Yield: 6 servings

1 cup yellow cornmeal
½ cup all-purpose flour
2 teaspoons baking powder
½ teaspoon soda
1 teaspoon salt
2 tablespoons finely chopped green onions (tops will add color)
1 tablespoon finely chopped jalapeño pepper (seeds and all)
½ cup cooked, crumbled bacon (fatty bacon is best)
⅔ cup buttermilk
1 egg
Peanut or vegetable oil

Combine all ingredients except egg and oil in a large mixing bowl. Separate egg yolk and white and add yolk to batter. Mix well. Beat egg white until stiff and fold gently into batter.

Pour 3 inches of oil in a medium saucepan or deep-fat fryer. Heat to 370°. Dip batter by small teaspoonfuls, using another teaspoon to push batter into hot oil. Cook for 3-5 minutes or until golden brown. Drain on paper towels and serve while hot.

A sack of corn saved John Wahrenberger's life in 1840. One evening while walking home from Austin's only grist mill with a sack of cornmeal slung over his back, Wahrenberger was attacked by Indians. Unarmed, he ran for his life, still carrying the meal. It's fortunate he did, for the flying arrows lodged in the sack instead of in his back. He made it to his house, where the Indians were fought off by other members of the household. Unhurt except for a wound to his arm, he caught his breath and exclaimed, "Oh meine Gott, what a Texas dis is, I think I go back to Switzerland!" But he didn't, and he became a respected citizen of Austin.

Totally Texas Cornbread

Tasty—and practically a meal in itself.

Yield: 6 servings

1 cup cornmeal
1 teaspoon salt
1 teaspoon soda
1 cup buttermilk
2 eggs
⅓ cup melted bacon grease or shortening
1 8¾-ounce can cream-style corn
2 cloves garlic, chopped
5 jalapeño peppers, seeded and chopped
1 medium onion, chopped
½ pound grated Cheddar cheese
1 pound ground beef, browned and drained

Stir first 6 ingredients together. Add corn, garlic, jalapeño peppers and onion, mixing well. Stir in cheese. Lightly grease a 9x12-inch pan and spread with half of batter. Spread ground beef evenly over first layer of batter. Spread remaining batter over ground beef. Bake at 325° for 1 hour. Cool and cut into squares.

Breads and Breakfasts

In 1821 Moses and Stephen F. Austin received permission from the Mexican government to settle 300 European families in Texas. Every colonist was required to prove that "his character was perfectly unblemished, that he was a moral and industrious man, and absolutely free from the vice of intoxication." By 1827 all but 3 of the titles had been issued. In 1829 Stephen Austin wrote of his colony on the Brazos River, "you will be astonished to see all our houses with no other fastening than a wooden pin or door latch." The "Old Three Hundred," as the colonizing families came to be called, are as revered in the state as the Pilgrims of New England are in the United States.

Kay's Bran Muffins

Wonderful, moist muffins that will delight anyone you decide to share them with. If the batter is kept refrigerated, you can have two or three batches of fresh hot muffins for breakfast.

Yield: 4 dozen

3 cups sugar
5 cups flour
5 teaspoons soda
2 teaspoons salt
4 eggs, beaten
1 quart buttermilk
1 cup vegetable oil
1½ cups raisins
1 cup chopped walnuts
   or pecans
1 15-ounce box raisin
   bran cereal

Combine sugar, flour, soda and salt in a large bowl. Add eggs, buttermilk and oil. Mix well. Add remaining ingredients and stir. Fill greased muffin tins two-thirds full and bake at 400° for 20-25 minutes. If you decide to bake only part of the batter, cover and refrigerate remainder for up to 6 weeks.

Breads and Breakfasts

On a scenic bluff overlooking the Colorado River near La Grange in Fayette County an angel on a 48-foot granite monument keeps watch over the tomb of 52 Texas patriots killed in battle with Mexico some six years after the Battle of San Jacinto. Thirty-six were slain in the Dawson Massacre at Salado Creek as they marched to protect San Antonio. The others are heroes of the "black bean lottery," their fate determined by Santa Anna's order that every 10th prisoner of the 1843 ill-fated Mier expedition be executed. Black and white beans were put into a pot, and prisoners drawing black ones were executed forthwith. In 1848 remains of both groups were given a military burial on the bluff, now designated Monument Hill State Historic Site.

Ave's Health Bread

This bread has a wonderful flavor, and it's good for you.

Yield: 2 loaves

1¾ cups scalded lowfat milk
1 cup oatmeal
3 tablespoons sugar
1 tablespoon dry yeast
(or more if you like a lighter loaf)
¼ cup warm water
½ cup corn oil
5 cups all-purpose flour
(approximately)
¼ cup wheat germ
2 teaspoons salt (optional)

Soak oatmeal in scalded milk; add sugar and cool. Dissolve yeast in warm water and combine with oatmeal and milk. Add corn oil and mix. Combine remaining ingredients and add one cup at a time to form a fairly stiff dough.

Turn out on a lightly floured surface and knead until dough is smooth. (If dough is sticky, add a little more flour.) Cover and let rise in a warm place until doubled in bulk. Punch down and divide into 2 loaves. Place in greased 9½x5½x2¾-inch loaf pans. Cover and let rise for about 1 hour. Bake at 375° for 30-35 minutes.

For early Texas housewives the usual challenge was to find *anything* to put on the table. They often had to resort to wild thistles and other native greens to accompany the wild game and fish their husbands brought in. When there was no meat, they would search nearby riverbeds — if they were lucky enough to live near a river — for fresh-water mussels which, when boiled for hours with cornmeal, made an edible soup. Small wonder one Texian housewife said, "Texas is heaven for men and dogs, but hell for women and oxen."

Susette's Spoon Bread

This is a side dish and is served with a spoon like a grits or rice dish. If you have any left over, slice and toast.

Yield: 6 servings

4 cups milk
1 cup cornmeal
2 tablespoons butter
2 eggs, beaten
1 teaspoon salt

Bring 2 cups milk to a boil in a medium saucepan. Add cornmeal and stir for 5 minutes over medium-low heat. Take from heat and add butter. Slowly blend in 1 cup cold milk. Add eggs, salt and remaining milk. Bake in a buttered 2-quart casserole for 50-60 minutes.

Variation: Instead of milk, you may use one 13-ounce can evaporated milk mixed with enough water to make 4 cups. For a richer spoonbread, increase number of eggs to 4.

The Central Texas Sausage Belt is Texas' most savory region, stretching east from Mason to Houston and north from Victoria to West. Within the belt are around 40 old-time meat markets, each of which makes its own sausages and smoked meats. German and Czech immigrants brought their sausage expertise with them, and soon the rest of us were hooked on the unique Ger-Tex-Mex flavor. The markets are run by people with names like Patek, Krause, Rabke, and Novosad, and most of the businesses have been in the families for generations.

Sue's Sausage Bread

This savory blend of sausage, cheese and ripe olives baked inside a loaf of bread is a special treat for casual entertaining, picnics or other moveable feasts.

Yield: 8-12 servings

1 package (three 1-pound loaves) of frozen bread dough
½ cup softened butter or margarine
1 pound grated Mozzarella cheese
1 pound grated Cheddar cheese
1 3-ounce can grated Parmesan cheese
1 4-ounce jar diced pimientos
2 4-ounce cans chopped black olives
1 pound bulk sausage, crumbled and browned
1 pound smoked link sausage, chopped and browned
Picante sauce to taste

Thaw bread enough to divide each loaf in half. Coat loaves with 2 tablespoons softened butter or margarine and let rise in a warm place for 1 hour. Combine remaining ingredients in a large bowl. Roll each half loaf into a 9x12-inch rectangle and brush with remaining softened butter. Divide sausage mixture into 6 equal parts, and spread lengthwise in center of each half loaf. Moisten edges of bread with water and pinch and pull together to seal. Put seam sides down about 3 inches apart on cookie sheets. Butter tops and let rise for 30 minutes. Bake at 350° for 25 minutes or until golden brown.

The Runaway Scrape was anything but dignified. When Texians heard of Santa Anna's invasion and the defeat of the Alamo early in 1836, they dropped everything and started running for Louisiana. It was the dead of winter and many were on foot. They faced flooding rivers, lack of food, separation from other members of their families, sickness and death. It ended only after the victory at San Jacinto and, even then, some of the runaways were slow to believe the good news and return to their homes.

Black-Eyed Pea-Zza Bread

Where could this recipe be from but Athens, the black-eyed pea capital of Texas. Jimmie Del Moore has won the prize at the annual Black-Eyed Pea Cook-Off several times; and when asked to send her very best recipe, she chose this one.

Yield: 6 servings

1 1-pound loaf frozen bread dough, thawed
2 egg yolks, beaten
3 cups cooked black-eyed peas, drained and mashed
1 package Pepperoni slices
1 pound bulk sausage, cooked and drained
½ cup chopped onion
1 cup grated Cheddar cheese
1 cup grated Mozzarella cheese

Let bread dough rise until double in bulk. Roll out in a rectangle on a floured surface. Brush with egg yolks. Spread remaining ingredients in order given. Roll up lengthwise, pinching and pulling bread dough so that all ingredients are encased. Roll onto a cookie sheet with seam side down and bake at 350° for 30 minutes. Serve on a long bread board. Slice into 1½-inch pieces.

Schulenburg Czech Kolaches

Yield: 3-4 servings

Step 1:

2 ¼-ounce packages dry yeast
1 cup warm milk (120°-130°)
2 cups all-purpose flour
2 cups sugar

Combine ingredients, beat well and let rise until doubled in bulk.

Step 2:

2 cups warm milk
¼ cup sugar
6 tablespoons shortening
1 cup cream
¾ cup evaporated milk
1 tablespoon salt
6-7 cups all-purpose flour
    Melted butter

Combine all ingredients and add to risen dough. Mix in well and knead with floured hands. Dough will be soft and sticky, not like bread dough. When flour is thoroughly mixed in, place in an oiled bowl and brush top with melted butter. Let rise until doubled in bulk.

Shape dough into 1½-inch balls. Place balls on a greased cookie sheet and let rise until light. Make a depression in center of each ball and fill with fruit or streusel filling. Bake at 400° for 15-20 minutes.

Fruit Filling: Cook 1 pound prunes or apricots until soft and remove from heat. Add ½ cup sugar and 1 teaspoon cinnamon and mix well.

Streusel Topping: Combine 2 cups sugar, 6 tablespoons flour and enough melted butter to make crumbly.

Breads and Breakfasts

Long before the Pilgrims gave thanks in 1620 for a safe landing at Plymouth Rock, a Thanksgiving service was held in the land destined to be Texas. While leading his men north from Mexico in 1541, Coronado came upon a tribe of Tejas Indians in Palo Duro Canyon who befriended the beleagured Spaniards and gave them food. The grateful Coronado ordered a day of feast and thanksgiving. A marker placed at the site in 1959 commemorating "Feast of First Thanksgiving - 1541 - Proclaimed by Padre Fray Juan de Padilla for Coronado and his troops in Palo Duro Canyon 79 years before the Pilgrims" was later destroyed by vandals. The historical marker now in the Canyon refers to the event as a legend.

Company Coffee Cake

A smooth, moist coffee cake.

Yield: 12 servings

1 cup margarine
2 cups sugar
2 eggs
2 cups flour
¼ teaspoon salt
1 teaspoon baking powder
1 cup sour cream
1 teaspoon vanilla
4 tablespoons brown sugar
4 teaspoons cinnamon
½ cup chopped nuts

Cream margarine, sugar and eggs in a large mixing bowl. Sift dry ingredients together and add alternately with sour cream. Stir in vanilla and mix well.

Pour half of batter into a greased and floured tube pan. Combine brown sugar, cinnamon and nuts and spread half over batter in pan. Add remaining batter and sprinkle with rest of the brown sugar mixture. Bake at 350° for 60-65 minutes.

The City of Houston's first professional theatrical performance in 1838, two plays presented by a traveling company, almost ended in a shootout. President Sam Houston's party was late in arriving, and in the meantime local gamblers had filled their reserved seats. The gamblers refused to get up when asked, so soldiers were called in. They were ready to fire when Houston walked in and restored the peace. The gamblers left after getting their money back, and Houston enjoyed the rest of the show without incident.

Blueberry Buckle

A wonderful coffee cake.

Yield: 9 servings

¾ cup sugar
¼ cup shortening
 1 egg
½ cup milk
 2 cups flour
 1 teaspoon salt
 2 teaspoons baking powder
 2 cups drained blueberries
     (frozen, canned or fresh)

Combine sugar, shortening and egg in a medium mixing bowl. Stir in milk. Sift flour with salt and baking powder and add to batter. Gently blend in berries. Spoon into a greased and floured 9-inch-square baking pan. Sprinkle with Crumb Topping and bake at 350° for 45-50 minutes.

Crumb topping:

½ cup sugar
⅓ cup flour
½ teaspoon cinnamon
¼ cup soft butter or margarine

Mix well and spread over blueberry batter before baking.

BREADS AND BREAKFASTS

Texas governors have been a motley crew, as diverse in makeup as the state they governed. The first assumed leadership in 1846 after Texas' 10-year stint as an independent nation. The top seat has been occupied since by some big men: one over 400 pounds, another over 300; many measured 6 feet-plus in their stockings. One supposedly never wore socks—and always rode a mule. One married for the third time at 87. Another led a hillbilly band. The only woman was actually surrogate governor for her impeached husband. Refusing to bow out, one barricaded himself inside the Capitol. The famous Sam Houston had also served as governor of Tennessee and president of The Republic of Texas.

Too-Easy-To-Be-Good Coffee Cake

Barbara Tompkins of Midland says this is a favorite to prepare ahead for Christmas morning. It is so easy to do and makes a luscious coffee cake with a finger-lickin' sticky topping.

Yield: 12 servings

1 25-ounce package frozen cloverleaf or parkerhouse rolls (24 count)
1 cup brown sugar
1 3⅝-ounce package butterscotch pudding and pie filling (regular, not instant)
½ cup chopped pecans
½ cup melted butter or margarine

Layer frozen rolls in a bundt pan. Mix brown sugar, butterscotch pudding and pecans and sprinkle on rolls. Pour butter or margarine over top. Cover with a dishtowel and let rise overnight at room temperature. Bake at 350° for 30-35 minutes. Let stand for 10 minutes after removing from oven; invert on a large round plate. Spoon any caramel mixture that runs on plate over top of rolls.

North Dallas Omelet

Yield: 2 servings

4 eggs
4 tablespoons butter or
   margarine
2 tablespoons diced onion
2 tablespoons chopped tomato
2 tablespoons diced zucchini
½ teaspoon seasoned salt
2 tablespoons cooking wine
½ cup grated Cheddar cheese

Break eggs into a medium bowl. Beat with a fork or whisk for 30 seconds and set aside. Heat 2 tablespoons butter or margarine in a medium skillet; add vegetables and seasoned salt and sauté until tender. Add wine and continue cooking for 1 minute. Drain vegetables, reserving liquid. Add liquid to eggs and beat for 15 seconds.

Melt 2 tablespoons butter or margarine in a non-stick, 10-inch skillet with sloping sides. Add egg mixture and cook without stirring over medium-low heat. As eggs begin to set, lift edges with a spatula so that uncooked eggs will run under the set portion when pan is tilted. Check bottom of eggs to make sure they do not brown. When eggs are set around the edges but creamy in the center, spoon vegetables down the middle and sprinkle grated cheese over top. Fold side of omelet over vegetables, slide omelet onto plate and serve with fresh fruit.

BREADS AND BREAKFASTS

In the forty years between 1821 and 1861 the flags of Spain, Mexico, the Republic of Texas, the United States and the Confederate States flew over Texas. One couple who lived during this era, John Litton and Sarah Standifer, were married five times — a new ceremony with each change in government — because Sarah wanted to run no risk regarding the legality of her marriage to John.

Peep's Puff Pancake with Blueberries

This baked pancake puffs up in the oven and is delicious for breakfast or as a dessert. It's easy enough for young cooks to enjoy making.

Yield: 4 servings

Pancake:

- 4 tablespoons butter or margarine
- ½ cup milk
- ½ cup all-purpose flour
- 2 tablespoons sugar
- ⅛ teaspoon cinnamon
- 2 eggs

Blueberry Topping:

- ¼ cup orange juice
- 1 tablespoon cornstarch
- 1 cup fresh or frozen blueberries
- ¼ cup brown sugar
- ¼ tablespoon vanilla

Melt butter in a 9-inch skillet or pie tin, tilting pan to coat sides. In a medium bowl whisk milk, flour, sugar, cinnamon and eggs. Pour into the skillet or pie tin. Bake at 425° for 20 minutes until puffed and golden. Serve with Blueberry Topping.

Mix a little orange juice with cornstarch to dissolve. Combine with remaining juice and other ingredients in a medium saucepan and cook until thickened and clear. Spread over top of Puff Pancake and serve immediately.

Apple Fritters

A favorite family brunch, served with sausage and a big fruit plate.

Yield: 5-6 servings

1 cup all-purpose flour
1½ teaspoons baking powder
½ teaspoon salt
1 tablespoon sugar
½ cup milk
2 teaspoons corn oil
½ teaspoon vanilla
1 egg, slightly beaten
3 tart apples, chopped
 Oil or melted shortening for
 deep frying

Combine flour, baking powder, salt and sugar in a medium mixing bowl. Mix milk, oil, vanilla and egg and gradually blend into dry ingredients. Mix chopped apples into the batter. Heat oil or shortening in a medium saucepan to 350°. Drop batter by tablespoon into hot grease and fry for 3-5 minutes or until golden brown. Remove fritters with a slotted spoon and drain on paper towels. Serve with confectioners sugar and lemon wedges.

Pecan Waffles

Yield: 8 waffles

3 eggs
2 cups buttermilk
2 cups all-purpose flour
1 teaspoon baking soda
2 teaspoons baking powder
½ teaspoon salt
½ cup melted bacon grease
4 tablespoons chopped pecans

Beat eggs and buttermilk in a medium bowl. Sift dry ingredients together, add to egg mixture and beat. Mix in bacon grease. Pour about ¼ cup batter in a preheated waffle iron. Sprinkle ½ tablespoon pecans over batter and bake until almost no steam comes from waffle iron. Check waffle and remove when golden brown.

Brunch Casserole

This is a delicious casserole for breakfast or for a light supper, and it can be made the day before and refrigerated.

Yield: 12 servings

Sauce:

8 slices bacon, cooked and crumbled (reserve drippings)
¼ cup butter or margarine
2 2½-ounce packages pressed sliced beef
1 pound fresh mushrooms
¼ cup all-purpose flour
¼ teaspoon black pepper
3 cups milk

While bacon is draining on paper towels, melt butter or margarine with bacon drippings in a large skillet. Snip beef into small bite-size pieces with scissors and add to the skillet. Slice mushrooms in half and sauté with beef for 3 minutes. Add flour and pepper and stir. Gradually add milk, stirring until mixture begins to thicken. Add bacon and set aside.

Egg and Cheese Mixture:

16 eggs, slightly beaten
1 cup evaporated milk
1 teaspoon salt
½ cup butter or margarine
1 cup freshly grated Parmesan cheese
Parsley for garnish

Combine eggs, evaporated milk and salt and mix thoroughly. Melt butter or margarine in a large pan over medium low heat, add eggs and scramble gently until eggs are cooked but still moist. Oil a 3-quart casserole dish and add layers of sauce, eggs, sauce, cheese, eggs, sauce and cheese. Cover casserole dish tightly. Refrigerate until ready to cook. Heat 1 hour at 275°. Garnish with parsley.

Note: Grating fresh Parmesan cheese does take more time than using "store-bought" grated Parmesan, but will make a creamier casserole.

Breakfast Tacos

Roadside stands all over Texas advertise Breakfast Tacos. Scrambled eggs, sausage and seasonings are mixed together and rolled in tortillas for a delicious morning meal that can be eaten on the run. They are even better when made at home, topped with melted cheese and enjoyed in a leisurely fashion.

Yield: 4 servings

2½ tablespoons butter or margarine
1 small tomato, chopped
6 green onions, chopped
½ pound mild bulk sausage
6 eggs
¼ teaspoon pepper

1 tablespoon water
8 flour tortillas
1 cup grated sharp Cheddar cheese
Picante sauce
Avocado and orange slices

Melt 1 tablespoon of the butter or margarine in a medium skillet. Add tomato and onions and sauté until onions are soft. Remove from skillet and set aside. Crumble sausage into skillet and cook over medium heat until done. Remove sausage from skillet and add to tomato and onions.

Wipe skillet, add remaining butter or margarine and melt over medium-low heat. Mix eggs, salt, pepper and water, beating slightly. Cook in skillet, stirring slowly until eggs are set but still moist. Add sausage, tomato and onions and mix lightly.

Heat tortillas in microwave in a flat, covered microwaveable dish for 30 seconds. (Or wrap in foil and heat in a 350° oven for 10 minutes.) Place 2 tablespoons of the egg and sausage mixture in center of each tortilla, roll and place seam side down in a glass baking dish. Sprinkle with grated cheese.

Preheat oven to broil and place breakfast tacos under broiler just long enough to melt cheese. Serve with your favorite picante sauce and sliced oranges and avocados.

Tastes & Tales

SOUPS
AND SALADS

Texas Coast

The Father of Western Art was, appropriately, a Texan. As a youth, Frank Reaugh followed the great cattle drives up the Chisholm Trail, sketching all day beneath an umbrella and at night by moonlight. "No animal on earth has the beauty of the Texas steer," he proclaimed. At the 1893 Chicago World's Fair, Reaugh's Western paintings were exhibited along with those of other American and European masters. He painted longhorns and cowboys until he died in 1945 at age 85. The member artists of Kerrville's Cowboy Artists of America Museum continue to preserve Reaugh's rawhide legacy.

Teddi's Caesar Salad

Exactly the way a great tossed salad should taste.

Yield: 4-6 servings

Dressing:

- ½ **cup salad oil**
- ¼ **cup red wine vinegar**
- 2 **tablespoons Worcestershire sauce**
- 2 **cloves garlic, pressed**
- ¼ **teaspoon salt**
  Freshly ground pepper
- 1 **egg, beaten**

Combine all ingredients except egg 24 hours in advance. Refrigerate. When ready to serve add egg and whisk until mixed.

Salad Ingredients:

- 1 **head romaine lettuce**
- 2 **tablespoons grated Parmesan cheese**
- 2 **cups toasted croutons**

Separate leaves of romaine. Break the large leaves into fourths and the smaller leaves into halves. Wash carefully in cold water and drain well. Cover and refrigerate several hours. When ready to serve, place romaine in a large bowl, add cheese and croutons and enough dressing to coat greens. Toss thoroughly.

The Texas legislature once thought so little of the Panhandle's future that it swapped 10 counties (over 3 million acres) to pay for building the State Capitol. The land was sold to the British-financed "Capitol Syndicate," which determined that the land should be ranched until it could be subdivided for farming. So the XIT Ranch ("X" for the Syndicate's 10 members, "IT" for "in Texas") was short-lived; the Syndicate started selling off land in 1901 and sold the last of its cattle in 1912. Dalhart holds an annual XIT reunion, complete with a parade featuring a horse with an empty saddle, honoring the range riders of the past.

Leann's Special Salad

This salad recipe comes with a guarantee that there will be none left over. The toasted almonds are just the right touch with mushrooms and avocado.

Yield: 6-8 servings

1 **bunch red-leaf lettuce**
½ **bunch romaine lettuce**
½ **medium head iceburg lettuce or endive**
1 **large avocado, chopped**
½ **cup grated Romano cheese**
½ **cup sliced almonds, toasted**
1 **8-ounce package fresh mushrooms, sliced**
1 **6-ounce package Good Seasons Italian Dressing, prepared as directed**

Wash greens thoroughly, dry by patting with paper towels and refrigerate for several hours before serving. When ready to assemble salad, tear greens into bite-size pieces and place in a large salad bowl. Add remaining ingredients and toss well.

Spanish settlers first established a foothold in South Texas along the Rio Grande in the 1700's. Theoretically their land grants, or porciones, were all of the same size, but in reality they weren't. Porciones were measured with rawhide chains, and some of the settlers were smart enough to have their lands measured on wet days, when the rawhide would stretch far beyond its normal length.

Grapefruit-Avocado Salad

Yield: 6 servings

2 ripe avocados, peeled
   and sliced
   Lemon or lime juice
1 red grapefruit
1 small red onion, sliced
   and separated into rings
1 small head romaine lettuce,
   washed and torn into
   salad-size pieces
½ cup Honey-Celery Seed
   Dressing

Sprinkle lemon or lime juice on avocado slices; turn gently to coat. Peel grapefruit with a sharp knife to remove both outer and soft, white inner layers of skin. Cut out each section so it becomes a bite-size piece free of any peel or membrane. Combine avocado slices, grapefruit, onion rings and romaine in a medium salad bowl. Add dressing just before serving and toss gently.

Honey-Celery Seed Dressing:

3 tablespoons vinegar
3 tablespoons lemon juice
½ cup salad or peanut oil
3 tablespoons honey
1 teaspoon celery seed
½ teaspoon dry mustard
¼ teaspoon salt

Combine dressing ingredients in a pint jar and shake well. Use only as much as needed to lightly coat salad ingredients. Refrigerate remaining dressing for use another day.

Life is far-flung in Loving County, the least populous county in the state. It is bordered by New Mexico on the north, the Pecos River on the west and miles and miles of West Texas elsewhere. With fewer than 20 ranches and farms and a dwindling number of producing oil fields, neighbors in Loving County increasingly have elbow room. The population is below 100 and still dropping, giving it a population rating of .01 per square mile. (Dallas has 1,769 people per square mile.) Now you know where to go if you're looking for wide-open spaces.

Jicama-Orange-Onion Salad

Jicama is a crisp vegetable that looks like a turnip but tastes a little like a water chestnut. It is a great addition to salads and a favorite appetizer when cut into sticks and used for dipping dips.

Yield: 6 servings

1 small jicama, peeled
4 large seedless oranges
1 medium Spanish onion, thinly sliced
½ pound fresh spinach, washed and stemmed
½ cup corn or peanut oil
¼ cup white vinegar
1 tablespoon lime juice
½ teaspoon salt
¼ teaspoon cumin

Cut jicama into ¼-inch slices. Stack slices and cut into ½-inch strips. Peel oranges deeply enough to remove white membrane. Slice ½-inch thick and cut each orange slice in half. Separate onion slices into rings. Combine jicama sticks, orange slices, onion rings and spinach in a medium bowl.

Combine remaining ingredients and mix well. Add to jicama mixture 30 minutes before serving, toss and refrigerate. Serve in a glass salad bowl.

Residents of Corpus Christi got bombed in more ways than one by Yankee gunboats during the Battle of Corpus Christi in August 1862. Union sailors on one of the gunboats were in the process of pilfering a barrel of whiskey when they were ordered to open fire. To avoid detection they had replaced the gunpowder in some of their shells with the stolen whiskey. There was no time to change the "loaded" shells before the battle without revealing their theft; so, with profound regret, they fired away. A servant in town discovered that "whiskey bombs" were falling, and thereafter all was merry wherever they fell.

Water Street Seafood Company Avocado Dressing

This wonderful, creamy dressing is featured at the Water Street Seafood Company Restaurant in Corpus Christi.

Yield: 4 cups

2 cups mayonnaise	1½ teaspoons red wine vinegar
1 avocado, peeled, seeded and mashed	1½ teaspoons lemon juice
4 green onions, finely chopped	½ teaspoon salt
2 tablespoons minced anchovies	¼ teaspoon dry mustard
½ cup buttermilk	¼ teaspoon oregano
1½ teaspoons Tabasco sauce	¼ teaspoon white pepper
1 tablespoon Worcestershire sauce	¼ teaspoon celery seed
	¼ teaspoon garlic powder

Combine all ingredients in a large mixing bowl and mix well. Pour into a 1-quart jar and chill. Stir before mixing with chilled salad ingredients. Left-over dressing may be kept in the refrigerator for several days.

Garden Pasta Salad

Make this salad several hours before serving to allow flavors to blend.

Yield: 6 servings

1 10-ounce package
  spiral pasta
6 green onions, chopped
½ cup chopped cucumber
¾ cup broccoli florets
1 large carrot, cut into
  julienne strips
1 medium zucchini, sliced
½ cup sliced mushrooms

Cook spiral pasta in 4 quarts of salted, boiling water until tender (about 10 minutes). Drain and rinse in cool water. Combine vegetables with pasta and refrigerate.

Dressing:

¾ cup olive or salad oil
¼ cup wine vinegar
2 teaspoons lemon juice
2 cloves garlic, minced
1 teaspoon salt
2 teaspoons prepared mustard
1 teaspoon crushed dried basil
1 teaspoon dill weed
1 teaspoon celery salt
¼ teaspoon pepper
1 teaspoon sugar

Combine all ingredients in a pint jar. Shake to mix. Add to chilled pasta and vegetables. Refrigerate for several hours before tasting to correct final seasoning.

The Balcones Escarpment, a geologic fault zone, bisects Texas as it curves from Del Rio to the Red River. It rears up prominently northwest of San Antonio and rises just beyond Austin to a height of about 300 feet. To viewers on the plain below, the escarpment appears as a range of wooded hills several miles wide. It separates the Edwards Plateau, also known as the Hill Country, from the Coastal Plains. Its appearance prompted Spanish explorers to call it Los Balcones—the Balconies. The great artesian springs of Comal, Barton, and San Marcos as well as many smaller ones owe their existence to the fault.

Broccoli and Bacon Salad

This is an unusual and delicious combination of flavors. The salad may be prepared ahead of time if you hold the dressing until just before serving.

Yield: 6 servings

1 large head broccoli
½ cup raisins
¼-½ cup chopped onions
10 slices crisp bacon

Wash broccoli and drain. Remove and discard large stems. Slice or separate broccoli into florets. Place in a medium bowl and add raisins and onions. Crumble bacon on top.

Dressing:
1 cup mayonnaise
2 tablespoons vinegar
3-4 teaspoons sugar
1 cup sunflower seed kernels

Combine mayonnaise, vinegar and sugar. Add to broccoli mixture just before serving. Sprinkle sunflower seed kernels over all and toss.

During his sovereign reign in San Antonio's "Beantown" neighborhood and prior to his judging days in Langtry, Roy Bean ran a butcher shop of sorts. He would butcher "stray" cows and horses and sell the meat door-to-door or in the streets from a cart. He had a standing offer to pay $5 for any "stray" cow or horse brought him. His rationale? Why should poor folks go hungry when there were stray fat cows around? And he claimed that the minnows sometimes found in the milk he sold were there because his cows went down to the river to drink.

Crunchy Green Bean Salad

Yield: 8 servings

1 16-ounce can whole green beans
1 cup fresh bean sprouts
2 tablespoons sliced green olives
¼ red sweet pepper, cut in 2-inch strips
2 tablespoons sliced green onions
½ cup sliced celery
2 tablespoons sliced almonds, toasted

Drain beans and combine with remaining salad ingredients in a medium bowl.

Dressing:

¼ cup vegetable oil
2 tablespoons wine vinegar
1 teaspoon sugar
¼ teaspoon salt
½ teaspoon soy sauce

Combine dressing ingredients in a small jar and shake to blend thoroughly. Pour dressing over salad and chill for several hours.

Creamy Combination Salad

Looking for something a little different? This crunchy, creamy combination of flavors makes a great summer salad.

Yield: 4-6 servings

1 large cantaloupe
½ cup Wishbone French Dressing
3-4 very small cucumbers
½ cup pickling salt (or non-iodized regular salt)
1 8-ounce carton commercial sour cream

Pare cantaloupe and cut into bite-size pieces. Place in a medium bowl and toss with French Dressing. Marinate for 30 minutes. Wash small cucumbers, dry and slice in thin rounds. Place in a flat bowl and cover with salt. Let stand for 30 minutes. Drain dressing from cantaloupe and rinse and drain cucumbers. Fold cantaloupe and cucumbers into sour cream. Serve garnished with mint leaves in a pretty glass bowl.

Valley Coleslaw

Yield: 10-12 servings

1 medium head cabbage, shredded
1 green bell pepper, thinly sliced
1 large red onion, thinly sliced
1 cup vinegar
½ cup salad oil
½ cup sugar
2 teaspoons salt
2 teaspoons mustard seed
1 tablespoon celery seed

Combine cabbage, green pepper and onion in a large bowl. Bring remaining ingredients to a boil in a medium saucepan and pour over slaw while still hot. Toss and refrigerate for several hours or overnight for full flavor.

It is a delicious irony that some of the world's most flavorful honey comes from such desolate desert areas as Big Bend, where bees gather pollen from the blossoms of spiny trees and shrubs like mesquite, huisache, cenizo, huajillo, catsclaw and many varieties of cactus. Big Bend bees are quite well-travelled. Bee-owning ranchers often load their trucks with hives and "herd" their bees for miles and miles in search of desert blossoms.

Orange Blossom Salad

Yield: 10-12 servings

2 3-ounce packages orange gelatin
1 3-ounce package lemon gelatin
2 cups boiling water
2 cups ginger ale
1 cup canned pineapple tidbits (drain and reserve juice)
1 cup fresh sliced strawberries
1 cup mandarin oranges (drain and reserve juice)
2 cups diced bananas

Dissolve gelatins in boiling water. Add ginger ale. Pour into a 9x13-inch baking dish and cool. Add fruit, stir and let set until gelatin is firm but top is still "tacky" so that topping will adhere to base.

Topping:

½ cup mixed pineapple and mandarin orange juice
1 3-ounce package lemon gelatin
¾ cup sugar
1 teaspoon vanilla
1 cup sour cream

Bring fruit juice to a boil, add gelatin and sugar and stir until dissolved. Add vanilla and sour cream. Mixture will seem thin, but pour over gelatin base and refrigerate until set.

When all else fails, here are some old East Texas folk remedies:

To keep hawks from catching your chickens, nail a horseshoe over your fireplace.

To cure warts, steal someone's dishrag and never tell anyone where you hid it.

To cure the rheumatism, tie a string dipped in kerosene around your ankle.

To ward off ghosts and witches, men should turn all their pockets inside out at night.

Strawberry Pretzel Salad

Yield: 10 servings

Crust:

- 2 cups crushed pretzels
- ¾ cup melted margarine
- 3 tablespoons sugar

Mix ingredients and press evenly in a 9x13-inch baking dish. Bake at 400° for 8 minutes. Cool.

Filling:

- 1 8-ounce package softened cream cheese
- ¾ cup sugar
- 1 8-ounce container non-dairy whipped topping
- 1 6-ounce package strawberry gelatin
- 2 cups boiling water
- 2 10-ounce packages frozen strawberries, partially thawed

Mix cream cheese, sugar, and non-dairy whipped topping until smooth. Spread over top of pretzel crust.

Dissolve strawberry gelatin in boiling water and add strawberries. Let stand for 15 minutes or until cooled. Pour over cream cheese mixture. Chill until firm (about 2-3 hours). Serve and enjoy!

Many of our Christmas traditions were brought to Texas by the Germans who settled here in the 1840's and 1850's. Until they arrived, the holiday was scarcely celebrated. One pioneer remembers: "The cedar tree from the family ranch stood ablaze with candles in tin holders that had come from Germany. The tree bore cookies covered with glittering colored sugar and baked with hooks in them; oranges and apples and porous net stockings holding hard candies hung on many limbs. The 24th was a night of great activity. Supper was early—there was homemade wine, herring salad, and black-eyed peas for good luck, as well as the usual bountiful repast."

Mimi's Potato Salad

A creamy salad that grandchildren, grown children and all the cousins love. Potatoes should be cooked the day before making the salad.

Yield: 8 servings

8 medium potatoes
1 cup mayonnaise
2 tablespoons cider vinegar
½ teaspoon celery salt
½ teaspoon onion salt
½ teaspoon onion juice
6 hard-boiled eggs
1 medium Spanish onion, sliced

The day before you want to serve the salad wash potatoes and cook until they can be pierced with a fork. Cool overnight. Peel potatoes and cut into small chunks. Combine mayonnaise, vinegar and seasonings and mix with potatoes. Add sliced eggs and toss lightly. Place in serving bowl. Separate onion rings and overlap on top of salad.

Variation: Chopped green onions, sliced stuffed olives and chopped dill pickles are all good and can be used to vary the basic recipe.

Conrad Hilton came to Cisco, a small town 100 miles west of Fort Worth, in 1919 to buy a bank, but he had trouble finding a hotel room. Because of the oil boom, the only hotel was sleeping guests in 8-hour shifts round the clock. Hilton decided on the spot that the hotel business had more possibilities than did banking, so he bought the Mobley, a small, 2-story brick hotel. Later he wrote in his autobiography: "The Mobley, my first love, was a great lady . . . She taught us the way to promotion and pay, plus a lot about running hotels." Within 5 years he owned hotels in Fort Worth and Dallas, and the world's largest chain of hotels began.

Cisco Kraut Salad

Yield: 8 servings

1 16-ounce can sauerkraut
4 tablespoons pimientos
2 cups grated carrots
1 cup thinly sliced green bell pepper
2 cups thinly sliced onion
2 cups chopped celery

Drain sauerkraut well. Combine with pimientos and vegetables in a large bowl.

Dressing:

¾ cup corn oil
¼ cup cider vinegar
1-2 cups sugar
½ teaspoon salt
½ teaspoon celery seed
1 tablespoon cinnamon
Black pepper

Combine oil and vinegar in a medium bowl. Add sugar until you have the amount of sweetness you prefer. Mix in seasonings and stir until sugar is dissolved. Pour over vegetable mixture and let stand at room temperature for several hours. Chill before serving. This can be kept in the refrigerator for up to a month.

Strange as it sounds, the east Texas town of Marshall was once the capital of Missouri. When Yankee troops drove the Confederate Government out of Missouri in 1861, the governor and other state officials set themselves up in exile, first in Little Rock, Arkansas, then in Marshall. Rented houses served as their statehouse, governor's mansion and state offices. They were able to return home in June 1865. Marshall was a center of the Confederacy west of the Mississippi; and rather than surrender when the Civil War ended, a number of high-ranking Confederate officials headquartered in Marshall went to Mexico.

Chicken-Stuffed Tomatoes

Serve for a luncheon or a light summer supper.

Yield: 4 servings

4 large ripe tomatoes, peeled
3 cups cubed cooked chicken
¼ cup finely chopped celery
4 green onions,
   finely chopped
2 hard-boiled eggs, chopped
2 tablespoons sweet-pickle
   relish
½ cup mayonnaise
2 tablespoons sour cream
1 teaspoon seasoned salt
   Salt and pepper
   Salad greens (romaine,
   iceberg lettuce or endive)

Remove pulp from tomatoes to form ½-inch tomato shells. Turn shells upside down on paper towels to drain. Combine chicken, celery, onions, eggs and relish in a medium bowl. Mix mayonnaise, sour cream and seasoned salt and add to chicken mixture. Toss lightly until mixed. Add salt and pepper to taste. Fill tomatoes with chicken salad and serve garnished with salad greens.

Tip: To peel a tomato easily, place on a slotted spoon and immerse in boiling water for a few seconds. If tomato is ripe, 5-10 seconds is long enough; if not fully ripe, allow more time. Use a small paring knife to pull skin off easily.

Chicken in Lettuce Leaves
(Southwestern Style)

Bert Weigler is an innovative cooking instructor in Austin. This is her adaptation of an old recipe.

Yield: 6 servings

2 heads iceberg lettuce
1½ cups chopped onion
¾ cup chopped red bell pepper
6 tablespoons butter or margarine
3 canned jalapeño peppers, seeded, washed and finely chopped
1 small fresh jalapeño pepper, seeded and finely chopped
3 cups diced cooked chicken
1½ cups cooked rice
1½ teaspoons dried basil
A few grinds of black pepper
Salt to taste
½ cup chicken broth (or less — the mixture should be moist but not soupy)

Wash and separate lettuce so that leaves remain whole. Refrigerate. Sauté onion and red bell pepper in butter or margarine in a large skillet until barely tender. Add remaining ingredients, toss well, cover and simmer for 5 minutes. Arrange on a long serving dish with chicken mixture on one end and lettuce leaves on the other. Serve by spooning chicken mixture across the center of a lettuce leaf and rolling the leaf so filling is enclosed. Have each guest prepare their own and eat as a finger food.

The "dogtrot," a double log cabin popular in the early years of Texas' history, was the logical extension of the single-room log cabin. The builder just added a second cabin about 15 feet away from the first, then covered both cabins and the passageway, or "dog run," with a gabled roof. The "dog run" provided shade and caught the breeze while serving as a catchall for farm and household articles. It was also the favored sleeping place for the dogs.

Broccoli-Cheese Soup

Yield: 6 servings

1 10-ounce package frozen broccoli
1 cup thinly sliced carrots
1 cup finely chopped celery
3½ cups chicken broth
3 tablespoons butter or margarine
½ cup chopped onion
2 tablespoons finely chopped parsley
1 teaspoon garlic powder
¼ cup all-purpose flour
3 cups milk
1½ cups grated American cheese
½ cup sour cream
½ teaspoon Tabasco
Salt and pepper

Steam broccoli, carrots and celery until tender. Purée in blender or food processor with 1½ cups chicken broth. Pour into a large saucepan and add remaining 2 cups chicken broth.

Melt butter in a medium skillet, add onion and parsley and sauté until onion is transparent. Add garlic powder and flour and cook over medium heat for 3 minutes. Add milk gradually, stirring until smooth. Combine with vegetables and broth in the saucepan and cook over low heat for 30 minutes. Stir in grated cheese, sour cream and Tabasco. Salt and pepper to taste.

Boston has its Paul Revere and Austin has its Angelina Eberly. When Sam Houston, determined to create a new capital of Texas near the Coast, sent his men to rob Austin of the national archives on New Year's Eve 1842, legend has it the wide-awake Mrs. Eberly saw them, rushed to the nearby cannon on Commerce Street and fired it, arousing the local populace. An Austin posse recaptured the government's paperwork near Round Rock, and Austin remained the Capital of Texas.

Shirley's Soup

This delicious soup uses canned ingredients to save time but tastes as though you've worked hours getting that wonderful homemade flavor.

Yield: 8 servings

2 chicken breasts
   Water to cover
1½ cups salted water
¼ cup spiral macaroni
¾ cup chopped onion
1½ cups chopped celery
½ cup chopped green pepper
1 10¾-ounce can cream of chicken soup
1 10¾-ounce can chunky home-style chicken soup with vegetables
1 14½-ounce can stewed tomatoes
2 cups reserved chicken broth

Cook chicken breasts in water until tender (20-30 minutes). Drain chicken, reserving broth. Skin and bone chicken and cut into small chunks. Bring salted water to a boil and add spiral macaroni. Simmer for 8 minutes; drain. Combine macaroni and chicken in large pot or kettle and add remaining ingredients. Simmer over low heat for 20 minutes or until vegetables are tender.

The Old West flavor of the town of Bandera is reason enough for it to be called "Cowboy Capital of the World." The Hill Country town is also known as the Dude Ranch Capital of Texas. The dude ranch industry dates to 1920, when some Houstonians engaged bed and breakfast for several weeks at the Buck Ranch. After a great time riding horses and living the ranch life, they told city friends about their vacation find; and in 1921 several more groups came. The Bucks added rooms to their ranch house, and other ranchers started opening their homes and stables to visitors. Ranching and tourism are now Bandera County's biggest industries.

Cowboy Soup

This easy recipe has been tested on cowboys ranging in age from 4 to 70, and they all love it.

Yield: 6 servings

1 pound ground beef
1 medium onion
1 16-ounce can mixed vegetables
1 10-ounce can Rotel tomatoes and green chiles (or less if you prefer the soup not so hot)
1 13-ounce can Spanish rice
1 14½-ounce can stewed tomatoes
1 17-ounce can cream-style corn

Brown ground beef and onion lightly in a 4-quart kettle. Add remaining ingredients, cover and simmer for 40 minutes.

Soups and Salads

Bosque County in central Texas has been the hub of Norwegian culture in Texas ever since Cleng Peerson, recognized in both Norway and the U.S. as "the father of Norse immigration to America," led a group of immigrants there in 1854. Nowadays Norwegian traditions are carried on with an annual smorgasbord in November at Our Savior's Lutheran Church in Norse, where local ladies dress in Norwegian drakt costumes for the occasion; and every December the Texas Norwegians hold an authentic lutefisk dinner at Cranfills Gap. King Olaf V of Norway put this bit of Texas on his itinerary when he visited the U.S. in 1982.

Sot Suppe (Sweet Soup)

A traditional Norwegian food served on special occasions and especially during the Christmas holiday season. The recipe is from Teen Darden of Clifton.

Yield: 1 gallon

14 cups water
30 pitted prunes
2¼ cups sugar
½ teaspoon salt
4 sticks cinnamon
40 cloves
1 cup currants
1 cup raisins
4 cups water
½ cup tapioca
4 cups grape juice
½ cup lemon juice
1½ cups apricot nectar
1 cup port wine (optional)

Combine water, prunes, sugar and salt in a large kettle. Make a small cloth pouch for cinnamon and cloves (or use a tea ball) and add to kettle. Simmer over medium heat until prunes are tender. Remove prunes and spices with a slotted spoon.

Boil currants in 2 cups water until tender and add to kettle. Boil raisins in 2 cups water, drain, and add raisin liquid to kettle. Add tapioca; simmer and stir for 15 minutes. Add grape juice. Heat to boiling. Remove from heat; add lemon juice and apricot nectar and serve immediately.

The rough country around Junction was a favorite outlaw haunt on the Texas frontier. In 1877 Captain John B. Jones of the Texas Rangers ordered a "round-up" of Kimble County. His Rangers combed every draw and literally herded every man—good and bad—into a mesquite flat near Junction. Then the Rangers "cut the herd" just as if the men were cattle. The good men were set free and the bad were escorted to the county seat, where they were chained to trees until they could be tried, there being neither courthouse nor jail at the time.

Split Pea Soup with Ham

This down-home recipe is a favorite way to use the ham bone with all its tender morsels and flavor when there's no longer enough ham to slice.

Yield: 8 servings

2 cups dried split peas
7-8 cups cold water
    Ham bone, the meatier
    the better
2 cloves garlic, minced
½ cup chopped celery
1 medium onion, chopped
1 large carrot, sliced
2 teaspoons salt
    Pepper to taste
    Toasted croutons

Wash and pick peas. Place in a large kettle with 7 cups water. Add remaining ingredients and bring to a boil over medium heat. Lower heat, cover and simmer for 1½ hours. Remove ham bone and set aside. Purée soup briefly in a food processor or blender. Return soup to the kettle for final heating. If soup is thicker than you like, add more water. Pull all the meat from the ham bone and add to soup. Ladle into individual bowls and top with toasted croutons.

Tastes & Tales

MAIN DISHES

The Alamo, San Antonio

Main Dishes

Rancher versus farmer was a feud played out all over Texas. In Borden County in West Texas, the ranchers won. In 1902 large sections of the county's public land went up for sale, and prospective buyers quickly lined up outside the county clerk's door. Cattlemen, who were already established in the county, ordered their cowboys to yank out of line any and all suspected farmers. These "shirt-pullings" resulted in some serious fights, but the ranchers won and Borden has stayed strictly a cow county.

Marv's Grilled Chuck Roast

The wonderful flavor and tenderness of the meat comes from the beer marinade and method of cooking—better than steak.

Yield: 6 servings

3 pounds boneless chuck roast about 3 inches thick
8 ounces beer
¼ cup peanut oil
1 tablespoon soy sauce
1 tablespoon wine vinegar
2 cloves minced garlic
¼ cup minced onion
1 teaspoon salt
½ teaspoon black pepper
¼ teaspoon liquid smoke

Trim roast and place in a glass dish. Combine remaining ingredients in a medium saucepan and simmer for 10 minutes. Puncture roast every half inch with tines of a fork. Spoon marinade over meat, rubbing with back of spoon so that marinade seeps into small holes. Turn roast and repeat procedure. Pour any remaining marinade over meat and refrigerate for 4-6 hours, basting every hour.

To cook, place meat on grill over medium coals. Cook for 15 minutes, turn and baste with marinade. Cover grill and continue to cook for about 35 minutes, basting frequently with sauce. Check bottom side when basting and turn again to brown meat evenly. When meat is done to your liking, remove to carving board and let stand for 5-10 minutes. Carve meat against the grain in ½-inch slices. Serve with meat juices and any remaining marinade.

Main Dishes

Indescribable is the word that best describes Texas weather. April showers are just as likely to show up in March or May and March winds stir things up long before or after their allotted time. The lion and the lamb do lie down together in Texas. Blue northers chase away warm sunny skies; sandstorms deposit West Texas topsoil on Central Texas; hurricanes, tornadoes, droughts, floods, blistering heat, and freezing cold all get into the meteorological act. Small wonder a popular old Texas saying allows that only newcomers or dern fools predict the weather. And a poll of new residents got the same resounding response to questions of what they liked most and least about Texas: the weather.

Steak and Biscuits

Yield: 4 servings

2 pounds round steak, 1-inch thick
Salt and pepper to taste
½ cup shortening or oil
½ cup flour

1 large onion, sliced (optional)
2 cans (10 count)
refrigerated biscuits

Cut steak into serving-size pieces and season with salt and pepper. Heat shortening or oil in a large cast-iron skillet. Dredge both sides of steak in flour and brown in shortening or oil.

Add sliced onion to the skillet after turning steaks (optional). Remove steak (and onion) from the skillet and place in a 9x13-inch baking pan. Add remaining flour to shortening or oil in the skillet and cook and stir over low heat until flour begins to brown. Gradually add water, stirring constantly, to make a smooth, thin gravy. (Gravy will continue to thicken as it cooks with steak.) Pour gravy over steak (and onion).

Cover pan with foil and bake at 350° for 1 hour. Test meat with a fork. If it is not tender, return for another 20 minutes. When tender, top with biscuits and brown at 400° until biscuits are golden brown. Serve with a vegetable and salad for a meal to please the men in your life.

Savory Beef in Red Wine

This is a wonderful recipe for entertaining. Serve it with fresh pasta seasoned with butter and chopped parsley.

Yield: 8 servings

6	slices bacon, chopped
3-4	pounds trimmed lean chuck cut in 1-inch cubes
2½	cups dry red wine
3	teaspoons instant beef bouillon
3	cups beef broth or stock
2	tablespoons tomato paste
4	cloves garlic, minced
½	teaspoon thyme
⅓	cup butter or margarine
⅓	cup all-purpose flour
4	tablespoons vegetable oil
4	tablespoons butter or margarine
20-24	small fresh white boiling onions
1	pound mushrooms

Cook bacon in a large skillet until transparent; remove from pan and set aside. Add meat to bacon drippings and sear over high heat until evenly browned. Place meat and bacon in a 4-quart casserole dish. Mix wine, bouillon, broth or stock, tomato paste, garlic and thyme. Pour over meat. Cover and cook in 325° oven for 2-3 hours.

Melt butter or margarine in a small saucepan; add flour, stir and cook over medium heat until browned. Mix slowly into broth in casserole dish and return to oven for 20 minutes.

Heat oil and butter or margarine in a large skillet. Add onions and sauté for 5 minutes. Cut mushrooms in half, add to onions and sauté for 2-3 minutes. Add onions and mushrooms to beef in casserole and cook for another 20 minutes.

MAIN DISHES

"Light as air, stronger than whiskey, cheaper than dirt," barbed wire salesman John Gates boasted in San Antonio in 1876. But nobody believed him, and his order book was empty. So he built a barbed wire corral in Military Plaza and invited skeptical cattlemen to bring him their "worst fence busters" so that he could prove "the cattle ain't born that can get through." The rambunctious herd charged the wire but backed off immediately, bellowing in pain and frustration. Twice more they charged before giving up. The crowd was convinced, and Gates spent the rest of the night writing orders.

Oven-Barbecued Ribs

Yield: 4 servings

3 pounds loin back ribs
1 tablespoon vegetable oil
2 cups sliced onions
2 cloves garlic, minced
½ cup vinegar
½ cup water
2 tablespoons lemon juice
2 tablespoons Worcestershire sauce
1½ teaspoons salt
1 teaspoon dry mustard
¼ cup chili sauce
3 tablespoons brown sugar

Cut ribs into serving-size pieces. Bake in a shallow pan at 450° for 30 minutes. While ribs are cooking, place oil in a large skillet and cook onions and garlic until barely tender. Add remaining ingredients and simmer for 10 minutes. Brush ribs with sauce. Lower heat to 350° and bake for 60 minutes, basting frequently. Serve with lemon wedges.

Betta's Beef Tenderloin

An elegant but easy recipe from the largest military base in the world, Ft. Hood.

Yield: 8 servings

1 4-5 pound whole beef tenderloin
3 tablespoons butter or margarine
½ cup chopped scallions or green onions
1 cup dry sherry
3 tablespoons soy sauce
2 teaspoons Dijon mustard

Coat tenderloin with 2 tablespoons of the butter or margarine. Place on rack in a shallow pan. Roast uncovered in a 400° oven for 20 minutes. While meat is roasting, sauté scallions or onions in remaining butter or margarine. Add other ingredients and heat. Pour over meat and roast for 20-25 minutes, basting frequently. Add a little water to juices and sauce in bottom of the pan, stir and pour over sliced tenderloin or pass in a sauce boat at the table.

Cheese-and-Onion Burgers

A special substitute for the ordinary hamburger.

Yield: 4 servings

1½ pounds lean ground beef
2 tablespoons water
2 teaspoons catsup
1 teaspoon Dijon mustard
½ teaspoon salt
¼ teaspoon pepper
4 small slices Cheddar cheese
Thin onion slices
Buns or large rolls, lightly toasted

Combine ground beef with water, catsup, mustard, salt and pepper. Divide into eighths and form into round 4-inch patties. Put cheese and thin onion slices on 4 of the patties. Top with another meat patty and seal edges to keep cheese from melting out. Cook slowly in a lightly oiled heavy pan until meat reaches desired degree of doneness. Place in toasted buns and serve with dill pickles and a salad.

Main Dishes

Lambshead Ranch has seen a lot of history since its beginnings in the late 1850's when the Matthews and Reynolds families joined a few other settlers on the Texas frontier. Indian raids continued in the area for the next decade. Once Indian camping grounds, the land has also housed a Comanche reservation, a U.S. fort commanded by Robert E. Lee and a stage station of the Butterfield Overland Mail. Watt Reynolds Matthews, 88, actively operates the family ranch. *Interwoven*, the personal story of frontier life by his mother, Sallie Reynolds Matthews, has become a Texas classic.

Calf's Head

A long-time favorite at Lambshead and other ranches. Early settlers in Texas firmly believed in "waste not, want not," so every bit of an animal was utilized. The recipe is printed as given us—and is one we did not test.

Yield: 6-10 servings

Dig a hole 18 inches deep and wide enough to accommodate head, allowing enough space for a good layer of coals. Build a big fire in hole and burn down to coals.

When head is cut off slaughtered calf, leave enough skin to wrap or fold over neck opening. Wrap head in wet burlap sack. Put a heavy wire securely around head—strong enough to lift cooked head from hole.

Shovel some coals out of hole, leaving a good layer on bottom. Place head in hole. Shovel live coals all around head and on top, then a layer of ashes on the top, followed by a good layer of dirt so that it is completely sealed off and no air can get in.

Let cook for 12 hours. Remove from hole by wire. Remove sack and skin and it's ready. All parts are there, cooked to a turn.

On ranches it is customary to kill a beef in the cool of the evening, so this procedure is usually done then and left to cook overnight. However, it can be done in early morning, cooked all day and eaten at night.

Main Dishes

In 1832 the Mexican Government, worried about all the American Protestants settling in Texas, was pleased to have a colony of Irish Catholics settle San Patricio in South Texas. The Mexicans held a 4-day fiesta in honor of the Irish and, at the same time, officially opened the new road from Matamoros to Goliad. One of the villages on the road was named Banquete, Spanish for banquet, to commemorate the festive occasion.

Corned Beef and Cabbage

This boiled dinner is a great St. Patrick's Day tradition that's too good to enjoy only once a year. It is easy, but does need long, slow cooking and good corned beef with seasonings.

Yield: 6-8 servings

1 4-pound package corned beef brisket with seasonings
Water to cover
4-5 medium potatoes, peeled and halved

6 carrots, halved
1 medium-size head of cabbage, cut into 8 wedges

Remove corned beef and seasonings from package and place in a large kettle. Cover with water, bring to a boil and cook for 5 minutes. Remove scum that will come to the top. Cover and simmer on low heat for about 4 hours or until tender when pierced with a fork. Remove corned beef from the kettle and place on a carving board or platter. Cover with foil to keep warm.

Add potatoes and carrots to water in the kettle and cook for 20 minutes. Add cabbage wedges and cook for another 10 minutes. Cabbage should be tender but not overcooked. Slice corned beef against the grain and center on a large platter; arrange vegetables around beef. Serve with Horseradish Sauce (see Index).

Variation: Corned beef may also be cooked in a 300° oven for 4 hours instead of on top of stove.

Main Dishes

Even seasoned frontiersmen got lost on the barren Texas High Plains, so early roads from one settlement to another were marked by a furrow plowed into the prairie sod. Ranchers carved roads to their ranch houses in the same manner. So scarce were landmarks that a lone, giant cottonwood tree standing in a pasture just north of Amarillo was known to every cowboy in the Panhandle. Its branches sheltered the yearly round-up headquarters of the Frying Pan Ranch.

Panhandle Sandwiches

Prepare these sandwiches ahead of time and freeze; then relax, knowing they may be heated as needed and that they will be enjoyed by whoever is lucky enough to be around to eat them.

Yield: 6 servings

¾ cup softened margarine
3 tablespoons prepared mustard
1 tablespoon Worcestershire sauce
6 green onions, finely chopped
6 French-style rolls (about 6 inches long)
6 slices Monterey Jack or Swiss cheese
¾ pound shaved ham

Combine margarine, mustard, Worcestershire sauce and onions. Split rolls lengthwise and spread both halves generously with margarine mixture. Cut cheese slices in half and place on bottom half of roll. Divide shaved ham equally and place on top of cheese. Put top half of roll on ham. Wrap each sandwich in foil. Bake at 350° for 5 minutes. If sandwiches are frozen, bake at 350° for 10-15 minutes.

Note: There are several good variations of this sandwich. Shaved roast beef or corned beef are both delicious. Poppy seeds may be added to margarine for additional flavor. Try whole wheat, onion or simple hamburger buns. Experiment!

Main Dishes

The Tigua Indians of Ysleta are Texas' oldest identifiable ethnic group, coming to the El Paso area in 1680 as refugees of the Pueblo Revolt in New Mexico. The nearby Hueco Tanks, now a state park, once belonged to them. The "tanks" are natural cisterns formed by depressions in limestone and usually hold water year-round. As the only water source for miles, the tanks attracted Pueblo Indians as early as 300-500 A.D. In Tigua legend, El Wiede, their Great Spirit, lived at the tanks and created the Tigua people there.

Tigua Award-Winning Red Chili

The restaurant at the fascinating Ysleta del Sur Pueblo Tigua Cultural Center in El Paso specializes in this chili. It is made with the red chile pods that are seen hanging on ristras in kitchens throughout the Southwest.

Yield: 10-12 servings

10-12 red chile pods
3 teaspoons lard
4 teaspoons salt
4 large garlic cloves, pressed
2½ pounds stew meat

¼ cup cooking oil
¼ cup finely chopped onion
1 teaspoon oregano
3-4 medium potatoes, chopped (optional)

Rinse chile pods, remove stems, shake out seeds and place in a large stew pan. Add 10-12 cups water and bring to a boil over medium heat (be sure all chiles are moistened). Place the chile pods in a food processor or blender with a little of the water they were boiled in. Process or liquify while adding remaining liquid from the pan. (Divide after adding 4 cups of liquid or your processor or blender bowl will become too full.) Continue to process until you have a smooth purée (3-5 minutes). Strain through a coarse strainer, and pour into a large kettle. Add lard, salt and garlic and simmer over low heat.

Brown stew meat in cooking oil in a large skillet. Add red chile purée and simmer for 5 minutes. Add onion, oregano and potatoes (if desired). Simmer for 30-45 minutes or until meat is tender.

Main Dishes

A meandering series of oyster reefs 2 to 3 feet beneath the surface of the water created a short cut across Nueces Bay from a point near Portland to the Corpus Christi side of the Bay, reducing a 40-mile trip to less than 8 miles. Indians used this reef crossing in their raids on the fishing village of Corpus Christi. In 1845 Indian fighter General Zachary Taylor, confident that he had a number of Indians trapped on a spit of land, decided to wait until morning for the attack. But when morning came the Indians had vanished. This event led to discovery of the oyster reef, which was later used as a wagon ford by early settlers until a causeway was built across the Bay.

Winter-Texan Chili

A satisfying chili recipe for those who prefer less "fire" than usually found in Texas chili con carne.

Yield: 6 servings

1½ pounds ground beef
1 medium onion, chopped
2 29-ounce cans tomatoes
2-3 tablespoons chili powder
2 16-ounce cans kidney beans
¼ pound grated Cheddar cheese
1 8-ounce carton sour cream

Brown ground beef and onion in a large skillet over medium heat. Drain well. Pour tomatoes into a large kettle; add meat and onion mixture and chili powder. Bring to a boil, cover and simmer for 1 hour. Add beans, cover and continue to simmer for 30 minutes.

Top each bowl of chili with grated Cheddar cheese and a generous spoonful of sour cream before serving.

Nancy Ann's Scrumptious Lasagna

Nancy Rector of Kerrville was a winner in the Seventeen Magazine *"Now You're Cooking" Contest for her menu that included this recipe.*

Yield: 12 servings

Meat for the Sauce:
- 1 pound ground beef
- 1 egg
- 2 tablespoons dried bread crumbs
- 1 tablespoon minced fresh parsley
- 3 tablespoons milk
- 1 teaspoon salt
- 1 clove garlic, minced
- 2 tablespoons Parmesan cheese
- 2 tablespoons olive oil

Sauce:
- 1 large onion, minced
- 2 16-ounce cans Italian tomatoes, drained
- 1 6-ounce can tomato paste
- ¼ cup water
- 2 teaspoons salt
- ¼ teaspoon dried basil
- 1 teaspoon sugar

Assembly:
- 1 16-ounce package lasagna noodles, cooked
- 1 15-ounce carton Ricotta cheese
- 1 pound Mozzarella cheese, sliced
- 1 cup grated Parmesan Cheese

Combine all ingredients, mix well, and shape into 6-8 meatballs. Heat oil in large skillet and brown meatballs. Remove from skillet and set aside.

Sauté onion in same oil used for browning meatballs. Strain through a sieve or a food mill. Combine meatballs, onion, tomatoes, tomato paste, water and seasonings in a large saucepan; cover and simmer for 45 minutes.

Oil a 9x14-inch pan or two 8x8-inch pans and cover bottom of pans with some of the sauce. Remove meatballs from saucepan and mash with a fork. Mix ¼ cup of sauce with Ricotta cheese and spread over meatballs. Layer noodles, meatballs, and Mozzarella and Parmesan cheeses. Repeat layering process, ending with noodles topped with sauce. Sprinkle with Parmesan cheese and bake at 350° for 25 minutes. Remove from oven and cover with a dishtowel. Let stand for 15 minutes.

Texas Hash

Yield: 6 servings

1 pound ground beef
2 cups chopped onion
1 green bell pepper, cut into thin strips
½ cup uncooked white rice
2 teaspoons chili pepper
2 teaspoons salt
Pepper to taste
1 16-ounce can tomatoes

Combine ground beef, onion and green pepper in a large skillet. Cook, stirring with a fork to crumble meat, until meat is lightly browned and vegetables are tender. Drain excess grease from the skillet. Stir in rice, chili pepper, salt and pepper. Add tomatoes and bring to a boil. Reduce heat, cover and simmer for 25-30 minutes or until rice is tender.

Variation: Add 6 slices crumbled crisp bacon to above recipe.

Beef and Cabbage Casserole

Yield: 6-8 servings

1 cup uncooked long-grain rice
1 pound ground beef
1 large onion, chopped
1 head cabbage, shredded
4 carrots, grated
¼ teaspoon black pepper
2½ teaspoons salt
2 10¾-ounce cans chicken broth
½ cup butter or margarine

Spread rice evenly in bottom of a 3-quart casserole dish. Brown ground beef and onion in a large skillet, stirring occasionally. Add cabbage, carrots, pepper and salt to ground beef and stir. Spread over rice. Pour chicken broth over mixture, cover and bake at 350° for 1 hour. When ready to serve, dot with butter and mix in gently.

Main Dishes

Like other early Texas characters, Judge Roy Bean was cut from a different bolt of cloth. At a time when most Anglo-Texans held their Mexican neighbors in contempt, Bean embraced the Hispanic culture with gusto. One of his favorite dishes was chili con carne—made with liver. Bean took delight in the fact that his last name also applied to Mexico's staple food, and he often referred to himself as "Frijole."

Beef and Bean Bake

Yield: 10 servings

1 pound ground beef
½ pound bacon, chopped
1 onion, chopped
1 16-ounce can pork and beans, undrained
1 15-ounce can kidney beans, undrained
1 15-ounce can butter beans, undrained
½ cup catsup
1 tablespoon vinegar
¾ cup brown sugar (or less)
1 teaspoon dry mustard
Salt and pepper to taste

Brown ground beef in a large skillet. Drain and set aside. Cook bacon and onion together until bacon begins to brown. Add ground beef and remaining ingredients. Transfer to a large casserole dish and bake at 350° for 1 hour.

Variation: *If you prefer a tangy taste in the beans, use only 1 tablespoon brown sugar. Also, garbanzo or lima beans may be added or substituted for one of the beans listed.*

Ground Beef Empanadas

Empanadas are light, flaky turnovers with an infinite variety of fillings. The pastry makes them easily transportable whether they are an appetizer, entrée or a dessert.

Yield: Approximately 10

Ground Beef Filling:

- **3 tablespoons vegetable oil**
- **1 cup minced onion**
- **½ pound ground beef**
- **¼ cup golden raisins**
- **¼ cup pine nuts (piñon nuts)**
- **¼ cup minced red pepper**
- **2 teaspoons salt**
- **½ teaspoon oregano**
- **½ teaspoon celery salt**
  Pepper to taste
- **2 hard-boiled eggs, finely chopped**
- **¼ cup sour cream**

Heat oil in a large skillet and sauté onion for 2 minutes. Add ground beef; cook and stir until lightly browned. Add remaining ingredients, except eggs and sour cream. Mix well and simmer briefly. Cool, add chopped eggs and sour cream. Mix gently.

Pastry:

- **½ cup softened margarine**
- **½ cup softened cream cheese**
- **1¾ cups flour**
- **½ teaspoon baking powder**
- **2 tablespoons ice water**
- **1 egg, beaten with
  ½ tablespoon water**

Blend margarine and cream cheese. Sift flour and baking powder together and cut into creamed mixture with a pastry blender. Add ice water and toss with a fork. Gather into a ball, cover and chill for 30 minutes.

Roll out on floured surface until very thin. Use a 5-inch lid or small bowl to cut out circles of dough. Rework scraps of dough to make as many pastry circles as possible.

Place a large spoonful of filling in center of each circle. Moisten edges of circle with egg mixture and carefully fold edges of pastry together, enclosing filling. Crimp edges to seal pastry, and place empanadas on an oiled cookie sheet. Brush with egg mixture and bake at 350° for 20 minutes.

It's been said that a goat can live on nothing and a man can live on goat. For the Mexicans who lived in Big Bend in pre-Park days, the goat (like the buffalo for Plains Indians) furnished many of the essentials for living, including meat and milk, hair from which blankets and rugs were woven, hide for shoes, water bags and twine. Infants' cradles were made from goat hide, the hairy side up for warmth. The goat's bladder, dyed with ground paint rock, made a big red balloon for baby when inflated. Even the bones were carved to make tools and children's toys.

Beef Enchilada Casserole

Yield: 4-6 servings

1½ pounds ground beef
½ cup chopped onion
2 cloves garlic, minced
1 teaspoon salt
1 1.25-ounce package Taco Seasoning Mix
1 8-ounce can tomato sauce
4 large corn tortillas
1 15-ounce can ranch style beans
½ pound American cheese
1 5-ounce can evaporated milk

Lightly brown beef in a large skillet. Add onion and garlic. Cook and stir until onion is translucent. Add salt, seasoning mix and tomato sauce and simmer for 5 minutes.

Place 1 tortilla in bottom of an oiled 2-quart casserole dish, spread with half of the beans and top with another tortilla. Spread half of the meat mixture over that tortilla. Repeat layering of tortillas, beans and meat, finishing with a tortilla on top.

Melt cheese in evaporated milk and pour over stacked tortillas. Bake covered at 325° for 25 minutes. Remove cover and bake for 15 minutes or until golden brown.

Pronto Chili Enchiladas

Easy to put together with a minimum of ingredients.

Yield: 4 servings

8 flour or corn tortillas
4 cups canned chili
¼ pound shredded Monterey
   Jack cheese

Soften tortillas by dipping in hot oil or heating in a microwave oven. Place 2 tablespoons chili in center of each tortilla, roll tortilla up and place seam side down in a 9x12-inch baking dish. Spoon remaining chili over rolled enchiladas. Sprinkle shredded cheese on top and bake at 350° for 25 minutes.

Tip: Packaged tortillas are heated before serving to make them flexible and tender. Traditionally, they are softened by dipping in hot oil or sauce. However, using your microwave or oven will save time and calories.

Microwave method: Dampen your hand and pat each side of tortilla. Wrap no more than 6 in a slightly damp napkin or paper towel. Microwave tortillas on High for 35 seconds.

Oven method: Wrap tortillas in foil and heat at 350° for 12-15 minutes.

Oil or sauce method: Place ½ inch oil or sauce in a 10-inch skillet and heat. Dip tortillas, one at a time, into skillet long enough to soften (about 30 seconds).

To keep tortillas warm for serving, wrap loosely in a cloth napkin or place in a warmed covered dish.

East of Amarillo near the Oklahoma border the town names take on a British flavor—Tweedy, Shamrock, Wellington, Clarendon, Aberdeen, and Giles. In 1883 a British syndicate headed by the Baron of Tweedmouth and the Earl of Aberdeen bought 235 sections of land and named it the Rockingchair Ranch. But scornful Texas cowboys called it Nobility Ranch, or the Kingdom of Remittance Men, because it became a refuge for the nobles' younger sons (who got little or no inheritance). Scattered throughout the ranch were the estates of its members. But the rich nobles were poor ranchers and their herds were quickly depleted by theft. Disgusted, they all soon returned to Great Britain, leaving only their names behind.

Pork Mandarin

This recipe came from a transplanted Texan who enjoys serving Texas food to friends in England.

Yield: 4 servings

1 pork tenderloin
(1½ pounds)
2 tablespoons all-purpose flour
½ teaspoon salt
¼ teaspoon black pepper
3 tablespoons vegetable oil
2 medium onions, chopped
1 11-ounce can mandarin oranges
Grated rind and juice of 1 orange
1 cup water
1 chicken bouillon cube
1 green bell pepper, sliced

Coat tenderloin with flour seasoned with salt and pepper. Pour oil into a large skillet and heat. Add tenderloin and brown on all sides. Transfer to a 3-quart casserole dish. Add onions to oil and sauté until transparent. Spoon around meat.

Drain juice from mandarin oranges into a medium saucepan (reserve orange sections for later). Add grated orange rind and juice, water, bouillon cube, and green pepper slices. Simmer for 5 minutes. Pour over meat and onions, cover and bake at 350° for 1½ hours. Spread orange slices over top of tenderloin and return to oven for 15 minutes. Serve with rice or noodles.

William Sydney Porter, who wrote under the name O. Henry, began his professional career in Austin. In 1894 and 1895 he wrote and published "The Rolling Stone," a humorous weekly. Porter wrote about what he knew best, which included drinking beer. Friends swore that he was the only man in town who could down a half-gallon of beer without removing the stein from his lips. And they claimed that he spent long hours in the Bismarck Saloon, seeking inspiration from long glasses of pilsner and caviar sandwiches. His research resulted in such poems as "Conviviality":

> *If there is a rosebud garden of girls*
> *In this wide world anywhere,*
> *They could have no charms for some of the men*
> *Like a buttercup garden of beer.*

Pork Chops with Rice

Yield: 4 servings

1 envelope dry onion
  soup mix
2½ cups water
1 cup uncooked rice
4 large loin pork chops,
  ¾-inch thick
  Salt, pepper and flour
2 tablespoons cooking oil
¾ cup chopped celery
2 large cloves garlic
2 tablespoons water

Combine onion soup mix and water in a medium saucepan and bring to a boil. Add rice, stirring once; cover and cook over medium-low heat for 20 minutes.

While rice is cooking, season pork chops with salt and pepper and dust with flour. Brown in hot oil in a large heavy skillet, remove and set aside. Add celery and garlic to skillet. Cook and stir for 1 minute. Add water and deglaze pan by scraping to loosen browned bits of chops. Add cooked rice, stir gently and transfer to a 2-quart baking dish. Place browned pork chops on top of rice, cover and bake at 350° for 30 minutes.

The Mexican holiday Cinco de Mayo celebrates the victory of Mexican troops commanded by native Texan General Ignacio Zaragoza over invading French forces at Puebla on May 5, 1862. General Zaragoza was born near Goliad in 1829 and moved with his soldier-father to Mexico after the Texas Revolution. He fought against Napoleon III's experienced French troops with a ragtag Mexican army and won. While it didn't win the war, this triumph was an immense boost to Mexico's morale and created one of the most colorful celebrations to be found in Texas.

Frijol con Puerco

This tasty Mexican recipe combines black beans and rice topped with Pico de Gallo. It makes a colorful combination.

Yield: 6-8 servings

1 cup (½ pound) black beans
4 cups water
1 pound cubed pork
4-8 cloves minced garlic
Salt
4 cups cooked rice

Wash and pick over beans. Simmer for 2 hours and add pork. Simmer for 1 hour, add salt to taste and cook until beans are tender. To serve, ladle beans and pork in a bowl, add rice and top it with the Pico de Gallo.

Pico de Gallo:

½ medium onion, chopped
1 medium tomato, chopped
1 handful fresh coriander
6 radishes, chopped
1 Serrano chile
1 tablespoon lemon juice
Salt and pepper

Combine Pico de Gallo ingredients and season to taste.

Fort Concho was established in 1867 near the junction of two branches of the Concho River. Early records at the San Angelo fort reveal that military food was monotonous and meager. A meal often consisted of coffee, bread and bacon; and there were many complaints about the "green" bacon and the "sour" bread. Holidays were usually better; and an old document gives the New Year's Eve menu in 1875 as "8 wild turkeys, boiled ham, venison, antelope and goose." It goes on to quote the "weary" wife of Commanding Officer Colonel Benjamin F. Grierson as saying, "I think it will be a long time before we get up such another supper."

San Angelo Lamb Stew

This Lamb Stew is the best—and it comes from the heart of the sheep country of Texas. The secret to its goodness is in the method.

Yield: 6-8 servings

Step 1:

3-4 **pounds lamb shoulder, cut in cubes or chunks**
Juice of 1 lemon
Water
3-4 **cloves garlic, chopped**
2 **chicken bouillon cubes**
3 **medium onions, sliced**
3-4 **potatoes, peeled and quartered**

Step 2:

Baby carrots
Small boiling onions
4-6 **new potatoes, peeled and quartered**
Lemon juice
Salt and pepper

Trim lamb and drizzle with lemon juice. Let stand for 5-10 minutes. Place lamb in a large kettle and cover with cold water. Bring to a boil and cook for 5 minutes. Remove from heat, drain and rinse lamb in cold water. Wash the kettle; return lamb to the clean pot and cover with cold water. Add garlic, bouillon cubes, onions and potatoes. Cover and simmer for 1½-2 hours. Remove vegetables and purée with a little of the lamb stock.

Return purée to kettle and add baby carrots, small onions and new potatoes. Cook until vegetables are tender. Taste and adjust seasoning with fresh lemon juice, salt and pepper.

Butterflied Leg of Lamb

This recipe from Sue Sims of San Angelo, one of the finest cooks in Texas, is a treasure because it is so delicious and yet so easy. Sue owns a kitchen-gourmet shop, has taught cooking classes and has taken instruction from some of the world's finest cooks.

Yield: 6 servings

1 3-4 pound leg of lamb, boned and butterflied
¼ cup *good* olive oil (unless it's fresh, use peanut oil)
Juice of 1-2 lemons
Salt to taste
Freshly grated black pepper
⅓ cup soft butter or margarine
¼ cup Dijon mustard
½ cup minced fresh mint

Trim lamb carefully. Pound with a wooden mallet until lamb is of even thickness. Brush on both sides with olive oil (or peanut oil) and drizzle with lemon juice. Sprinkle with salt and freshly grated pepper. Cover with plastic wrap and let stand at room temperature for 30-60 minutes.

While lamb marinates, make a paste of butter, Dijon mustard and freshly snipped mint.

Have your grill or oven broiler hot. Cook 4-6 inches from fire for 7-10 minutes. Turn meat and spread paste generously over cooked side of lamb. Cook for 8-10 minutes, depending on thickness of lamb and how rare you like your meat. For "just pink" try 10 minutes on each side. Serve and enjoy. After that first taste you'll add lamb to your grocery list more often.

The advent of the working woman led to the decline of the daytime "hen party," which early Texas author Amelia Barr described:

"If the day was hot, they arrived soon after nine, got quickly into loose garments and slippers, took out their tucking and palm leaf fans and subsided into rocking chairs. They could all talk well, and by noon, all were ready for the delicious dinner sure to be prepared . . . young chicken fried in butter, venison roasted with sweet herbs, the broiled breasts of quails, or if later in the season, a pot pie of wild turkey. If any lady could by good luck secure milk or cream for a tapioca pudding or a dish of custard, the occasion was memorable. About four they began to dress, because after half-past four the invasion of the male might be expected and it was a point of honor to throw a little mystery around these meetings."

Sewing Club Rice Casserole

From a group of ladies in Alvin who can sew and cook and talk and do all of them well.

Yield: 18 servings

2 tablespoons vegetable oil
2 pounds mild bulk sausage
1 green bell pepper, chopped
2 cups chopped celery
1½ cups chopped onion
1 cup slivered almonds
2 cups uncooked rice
3 packages Lipton Chicken Noodle Soup Mix (dry)
9½ cups boiling water

Place oil and sausage in a very large skillet or kettle. Cook, stirring to crumble sausage until no longer pink. Add green pepper, celery and onion. Continue cooking until vegetables are glossy. Add almonds, rice and dry soup mix. Pour boiling water over mixture and stir until thoroughly combined. Transfer to a 5-quart casserole dish or small roaster and bake at 350° for 1 hour. Stir several times while baking. Serve to a hungry crowd.

Skillet Supper

Few dishes are as quick and easy to prepare as this one—and the men in your house will love it.

Yield: 6 servings

1 medium cabbage, coarsely
  shredded
1 large onion, chopped
½ cup chopped green
  bell pepper
1 pound smoked sausage
  or kielbasa
¼ cup water
1 teaspoon salt
¼ teaspoon caraway seeds

Combine cabbage, onion and green bell pepper in a large skillet. Cut sausage diagonally into 1-inch chunks and combine with vegetables. Add water and seasonings. Cover and simmer for about 20 minutes, stirring occasionally.

Venison Meat Loaf

Yield: 6 servings

4 slices bread
  Milk
1½ pounds venison hamburger
2 eggs, well beaten
1 medium onion, chopped
2 cups tomatoes, drained
2 tablespoons Worcestershire
  Sauce
½ teaspoon celery salt
  Salt and pepper
2 slices bacon

Moisten bread with milk and tear into small pieces. Place in a large mixing bowl with remaining ingredients, except for bacon. Mix thoroughly. Form into loaf to fit a 1½-quart baking pan. Top with bacon strips. Bake at 350° for 1 hour.

Chicken and Wild Rice

Karey Bresenhan is best known in quilting circles as originator and coordinator of the annual Houston Quilt Festival. She is also a fine cook and shares this wonderful recipe with us.

Yield: 6 servings

2 whole chicken breasts
1 large onion, quartered
1 carrot, peeled and sliced
1 stalk celery, sliced
2 tablespoons salt
½ tablespoon dill weed
½ tablespoon cracked black pepper
1 cup uncooked wild rice
½ cup butter (do not substitute)
½ pound fresh mushrooms, halved
½ cup chopped onion
¼ cup flour
1½ cups light cream
1 2-ounce jar pimientos
2 tablespoons chopped parsley
Salt to taste
Sliced almonds

Place chicken, onion, carrot and celery in a large kettle. Cover with water and add salt, dill weed and pepper. Simmer gently for 1 hour. Remove chicken from kettle, cool, and cut into bite-size pieces. Strain broth and reserve, discarding vegetables. While chicken is simmering, cook wild rice in 3 cups salted water for 40 minutes. Remove from heat, allow to stand for 10 minutes and drain.

Heat butter in a large skillet, add mushrooms and sauté for 1-2 minutes. Use a slotted spoon to transfer mushrooms to a large measuring cup. Add enough reserved chicken broth to make 1½ cups. Add onion to butter in skillet and cook until translucent. Stir in flour and gradually add chicken broth and mushroom mixture. Add cream and cook over medium heat, stirring until thick. Remove from heat; add chicken, rice, pimientos, parsley and salt and mix well.

Pour into an oiled 2-quart casserole dish. You may refrigerate or freeze the casserole at this point. To cook, top with almonds and bake at 350° for 30 minutes.

One of Texas' oddest industries of this century was centered in the great white sand dunes around Monahans, an area often likened to the Sahara Desert. There desert fleas were captured to be trained for exhibition in the world's most pretentious flea circuses. Troops of strong, intelligent insects noted for their quick jumping ability were taught such tricks as pulling tiny wagons, and they became stars in the miniature circus performances. It was claimed that Monahans fleas were vastly more robust and more easily trained than were the comparatively anemic fleas of other regions.

Chicken Bundles

An elegant and delicious recipe that is easy to make. There is nothing complicated about using puff pastry sheets, and they add such a special touch.

Yield: 4 servings

1 17¼-ounce package frozen puff pastry sheets (Pepperidge Farm)
2 cooked chicken breasts, skinned and boned
2 tablespoons peanut oil
¼ cup chopped onion
¼ cup chopped mushrooms
½ cup sour cream
1½ teaspoons prepared mustard
½ teaspoon garlic salt
¾ teaspoon salt
¼ teaspoon pepper
¼ pound Monterey Jack cheese

Thaw puff pastry sheets until flexible. Chop chicken into small, bite-size pieces. Pour oil into a small skillet, heat and add onion and mushrooms. Sauté for 3-4 minutes. Mix sour cream, mustard and seasonings and add to onion and mushrooms.

Cut each pastry sheet in half. Place a mound of ¼ of the chicken in center of each sheet. Spoon skillet mixture over chicken. Slice cheese and place on top. Bring ends of puff pastry together over chicken and fold twice. Crimp sides of pastry to seal chicken mixture inside. Place on a lightly greased cookie sheet and bake at 350° for 20-25 minutes or until richly browned.

Main Dishes

West Texans only chuckle when strangers find their climate hard to take. After exploring the area in 1849 Capt. R. B. Macy emphatically stated, "This country is, and must remain, uninhabited forever." Those who proved him wrong developed a special sense of humor, as shown in this dust storm joke: "There was a prairie dog 20 feet in the air, trying to dig out." Or like when the stranger asked a West Texan, "Does the wind always blow this way?" The native replied, "No, sometimes it blows the other way." Or their method of forecasting the weather by a chain clamped to a fence post: if the chain blows horizontal, a normal day is predicted; but if the links begin to whip around, a little rough weather can be expected.

Chicken Spaghetti Supreme

Everyone who tasted this dish loved it. The next time you need a dish that can be prepared ahead, or even frozen, this is the answer.

Yield: 12 servings

3 whole chicken breasts, cooked
1 green bell pepper, finely chopped
3-4 stalks celery, chopped
2 cups chicken broth
1 12-ounce package spaghetti (use ready-cut or break into 2-inch pieces)
2 10¾-ounce cans cream of mushroom soup, undiluted

1 pound grated Velveeta cheese
1 2-ounce jar diced pimientos
¾ cup white wine
4 teaspoons parsley flakes
2 tablespoons dried Italian salad dressing mix
½ teaspoon Accent
Salt and pepper to taste
½ cup buttered bread crumbs

Remove skin and bone from cooked chicken and cut into bite-size pieces. (You'll have about 4 cups chicken.) Cook green pepper and celery in chicken broth until tender. Cook spaghetti in salted water according to instructions on package. Combine all ingredients except bread crumbs and butter and transfer into a 3-quart buttered casserole dish. Top with buttered bread crumbs and bake at 350° for 30 minutes or until bubbly.

Crunchy Almond Chicken

This good chicken stir-fry recipe may be varied by using snow peas instead of broccoli or walnuts instead of almonds.

Yield: 6 servings

Chicken and Marinade:

2 cups uncooked chicken, boned and skinned
2 tablespoons sherry
1 teaspoon salt
2 teaspoons soy sauce
½ teaspoon sugar
1 tablespoon cornstarch
1 egg white

Cut chicken into bite-size pieces. Mix marinade ingredients and pour over chicken. Marinate for 20 minutes.

Vegetables:

4 tablespoons vegetable oil
1 cup sliced celery
1 cup broccoli florets
½ cup sliced mushrooms
½ cup sliced water chestnuts
2 cloves garlic, minced
½ cup chicken broth
1 teaspoon cornstarch
½ cup almonds
½ teaspoon salt
½ teaspoon sugar

Heat 2 tablespoons oil in a large skillet. Sauté celery and broccoli over medium-high heat for 1 minute. Add mushrooms and water chestnuts and stir-fry for another minute. Remove vegetables from skillet and set aside.

Add remaining oil to skillet and heat. Add garlic and chicken with marinade sauce and cook until meat becomes white. Mix 2 teaspoons chicken broth with cornstarch and add with remaining chicken broth to chicken. Cook until mixture is thickened and clear. Add cooked vegetables, almonds, salt and sugar and heat. Serve with rice.

East Texas Chicken Stew

This old family favorite from Port Arthur comes with instructions on how to make a roux, the important base of almost all Creole and Cajun recipes and the secret to this recipe.

Yield: 8 servings

Roux:

- ½ **cup Crisco oil**
- 1 **cup all-purpose flour**
- 1 **large onion, chopped**
- 4-5 **large cloves garlic, finely chopped**

Chicken:

- 1 **4-6 pound stewing hen**
  Red pepper and salt to taste
- 4-5 **14½-ounce cans Swanson Chicken Broth**
- 2 **cups chopped celery**
- 1 **cup chopped green onion tops**
- 1 **cup finely chopped fresh parsley**

In a heavy pot (preferably an iron skillet) heat oil over low heat; add flour. Cook flour very slowly, stirring constantly. (A good roux must be cooked slowly to eliminate any floury taste and to insure uniformity of color, which should be a rich, dark brown.) Add onion and garlic and transfer to a large pot or kettle.

Season chicken pieces with red pepper and salt and add to roux. Mix in 4 cans chicken broth, celery and onion tops. Cook over low heat until hen is tender and gravy is thick. Add parsley and cook for another 5 minutes. If gravy is too thick, add more chicken broth. Serve over hot rice.

Chicken Fajitas

Fajitas, traditionally made from strips of beef skirt steaks, have become an increasingly popular Tex-Mex dish. Cooks have discovered that chicken prepared with a marinade and grilled also makes a delicious filling for tortillas.

Yield: 4 servings

4 chicken breast halves, skinned and boned
1 large onion, sliced
¼ cup soy sauce
1 teaspoon Worcestershire sauce
1 tablespoon vegetable oil
1 teaspoon freshly ground cumin
Tortillas, guacamole, sour cream, Cheddar cheese and salsa

Marinate chicken and onion in marinade of soy sauce, Worcestershire sauce, oil and cumin for 1 hour. Grill over charcoal fire for about 4 minutes on each side. (Place onions to outside as they will not need as much cooking time.) Brush with marinade before and after turning. Cut chicken into thin strips and separate onion into rings. Fold into warm tortillas and top with guacamole, sour cream, grated Cheddar cheese and salsa.

Tex-Mex Chicken Casserole

Delicious! Easy!

Yield: 8 servings

1 3-pound chicken, cooked
1 large onion, chopped
3 tablespoons chili powder
1 19-ounce can chili without beans
1 15-ounce can tamales, cut into chunks
1 17-ounce can cream-style corn
1 cup grated Longhorn cheese

Remove skin and bone from chicken. Cut chicken into chunks and arrange in bottom of a greased 9x13-inch baking dish. Sprinkle onion and chili powder evenly over chicken. Layer remaining ingredients in order given. Bake at 350° for 30 minutes or until bubbly.

Main Dishes

Although Texas wines are winning medals and acclaim, commercial wine-making in Texas is still considered a fairly new industry. Yet long before the Civil War, "Pecos wine and brandy," made from grapes grown in the Middle Valley of the Rio Grande between El Paso and Van Horn, were famous. For a time these wines, shipped down to Chihuahua, up through New Mexico and east over the Santa Fe Trail, constituted El Paso's chief source of income. Grapes of an Asiatic variety were said to have been introduced in the 1660's by the Franciscans who built the early missions there.

El Paso Chicken Enchiladas

Cooks in El Paso stack their enchiladas, while most of those in the rest of Texas roll them before covering with a sauce to bake. This recipe comes from Elouise Lanham Phelan, a descendant of the 16th governor of Texas and an El Paso resident.

Yield: 10 servings

2	10¾-ounce cans cream of chicken soup
2	cups evaporated milk
1	4-ounce can chopped green chiles
12-16	corn tortillas, torn in pieces
1	large chopped onion
4	cups cubed chicken or turkey
8	ounces grated American cheese

Mix soup, milk and chiles in a medium saucepan and heat. Line a greased 3-quart casserole dish with tortilla pieces and add onion, chicken or turkey, soup mixture and cheese. Add another layer of tortilla pieces, then other ingredients in same order as before. Bake at 350° for 30 minutes.

Main Dishes

Necessity is the mother of invention, and those early settlers who chose to brave life in the deserts of West Texas were ingenious in their use of the prickly plants which abounded there. Needle-pointed yucca leaves opened rattlesnake bite wounds and served as sewing needles. A syrup was made of boiled screwbeans. Mesquite beans were prepared and eaten in a variety of ways, as were the pads and fruit of the prickly pear cactus. Sotol and lecheguilla fiber doubled as twine, and long-pointed sotol leaves were utilized as roof thatching. The long, straight, slender branches of the ocotillo plant were used in building houses and picket fences.

Turkey Sandwich Casserole

A wonderful way to use left-over turkey.

Yield: 6 servings

6 slices white sandwich bread, buttered and toasted
Turkey slices to cover bread generously
9 slices bacon, cooked and crumbled
2 tablespoons butter or margarine
½ cup chopped onion
1 tablespoon flour
1 2.4-ounce box Lipton's Cream of Chicken Cup-a-Soup (4 envelopes)
½ teaspoon dry mustard
2½ cups milk
2 cups shredded Monterey Jack cheese

Place toast slices in a 9x13-inch buttered baking dish. Cover each slice with turkey and bacon crumbles. Melt butter or margarine in a medium skillet, add onion and sauté until tender. Remove onion from the skillet with a slotted spoon and spread over turkey and bacon.

Blend flour with butter or margarine in skillet and stir over medium heat for 1 minute. Mix in cream of chicken soup and dry mustard. Add milk slowly, stirring until sauce thickens. (Add a little water if you feel it is getting too thick.) Pour sauce over top of sandwiches. Top with grated cheese and bake at 350° until bubbly, about 15-20 minutes.

Main Dishes

The roadrunner, or paisano, is one of the Southwest's most delightful creatures. The fleet bird can be seen racing along roads at speeds up to 15 miles per hour, never rising more than a foot or two off the ground. According to a Mexican folktale, the proud and haughty paisano was punished by the eagle, monarch of all feathered creatures, for its vanity and was condemned to forever walk instead of fly.

Turkey Drumsticks Parmesan

This oven-fried turkey is equally good made with thighs or breasts. Increase cooking time accordingly.

Yield: 4 servings

6 turkey drumsticks
1½ cups buttermilk
½ cup melted margarine
1 cup grated Parmesan cheese
½ cup Pepperidge Farm Stuffing Mix, finely crushed
1 tablespoon wheat germ (optional)
1 teaspoon salt
¼ teaspoon black pepper
¼ teaspoon garlic powder

Remove skin from turkey legs and marinate them in buttermilk for several hours. Remove from buttermilk and drain on paper towels for a few minutes. Combine remaining ingredients in a flat plate or pie tin. Roll turkey legs in mixture and place in a baking dish. Bake at 375° for 60-70 minutes, basting every 15 minutes with margarine.

Variation: To make Oven-Fried Parmesan Chicken, follow above recipe, decreasing cooking time to 50 minutes.

MAIN DISHES

Indianola on Matagorda Bay once rivalled Galveston as Texas' most important port of entry. Established in 1844 as an immigrant camp for Germans brought to the Republic of Texas to settle farther inland, the place became a permanent home for the many German families who did not find the expected help and promised land awaiting them. Indianola became a thriving seaport, but was wiped out by devastating hurricanes in 1875 and 1886. The once-bustling port 200 miles south of Galveston is now mostly a cemetery, a park and a memory. (Brownson Malsch's *Indianola, The Mother of Western Texas* offers a comprehensive history of the town.)

DeSoto Doves

Hunter and recipe contributor Randy Speer says this is the way his group prepares doves after a day of hunting the "gray ghosts." Since they hunt until the sun goes down, then clean the doves, fire up the grill and prepare dinner, most dove hunters are starved and will eat 3-6 dove breasts each.

Yield: 3-4 servings

12 dove breasts
1 medium onion, sliced
1 green bell pepper, sliced
1 pound thick-sliced bacon
　Salt and pepper

Make a slit in each half of the dove breast. Insert an onion slice in the slit on one side of the breast and a green pepper slice in the other slit. Salt and pepper each breast and wrap with a strip of bacon. Fasten securely with a round toothpick. Cook over medium coals (preferably mesquite) on a covered grill with ventilation holes at minimum opening. Cook until bacon is crisp, turning once.

Carrabba's Italian Quail

Carrabba's Restaurant is one of Houston's most popular restaurants. You'll enjoy this sophisticated treatment of a favorite Texas game bird.

Yield: 4-6 servings

1 cup red wine vinegar
¼ cup balsamic vinegar
2 bay leaves
10 sage leaves
8 prepared quail
8 slices bacon

Combine vinegars, bay leaves, and 2 sage leaves. Place quail in a baking dish and pour marinade sauce over and around them. Refrigerate overnight.

Prepare quail for grilling by wrapping each quail with one strip bacon, placing a sage leaf between bacon and quail. Fasten bacon with a toothpick. Grill over medium coals for 20-25 minutes, turning to cook evenly.

Marsala Sauce for Quail:

6 ounces sweet Marsala wine
6 ounces chicken stock
1 teaspoon finely chopped shallots
1 teaspoon finely chopped garlic
6 ounces unsalted butter
Salt and pepper to taste

Combine Marsala wine, chicken stock, shallots, and garlic in a small saucepan. Reduce over medium heat until shallots and garlic are soft. Add butter, salt and pepper. Ladle Marsala Sauce over grilled quail and serve with a flourish. You'll love it.

Autumn Fruit Cornish Hens

The Cornish game hens develop a rich, brown glaze as they bake; and when garnished with plump, juicy apricots and prunes, they make a beautiful dish for an elegant dinner.

Yield: 8 servings

8 Cornish game hens
12 cloves garlic, minced
4 tablespoons oregano
1 cup red wine vinegar
½ cup olive oil
1 cup pitted prunes
1 cup dried apricots
1 cup pitted green olives
½ cup capers with juice
   (3¼-ounce jar)
8 bay leaves
½ teaspoon salt
¼ teaspoon pepper
¾ cup white wine
½ cup brown sugar

Remove giblets and save for another day. Rinse hens and pat dry. Trim any bits of fat skin if necessary. Combine remaining ingredients, *except* wine and brown sugar, and pour over hens. Cover and refrigerate overnight, basting with marinade occasionally.

When ready to cook, arrange hens in a shallow roasting pan. Add wine to marinade and baste hens. Spoon fruit, olives, capers and marinade around hens. Sprinkle brown sugar evenly over hens. Do not disturb brown sugar while hens are baking as it forms a beautiful rich, brown glaze.

Bake in preheated 350° oven for 1 hour and 15 minutes or until a leg moves easily when pressed. Spoon marinade over top of hens to moisten. Serve hens surrounded by fruit and parsley on a large tray.

Main Dishes

General Jonathan "Skinny" Wainwright, a hero in World War II, was born in Washington state but saw his first battle as a cavalry officer on the Texas Rio Grande border in the early 1900's. The outbreak of WW II found him on the border at Brackettville, and he was sent to the Phillipines. Douglas MacArthur left Wainwright to continue the defense of the islands, which he later had to surrender to the Japanese. Wainwright spent three and a half years in Japanese prison camps and received the Medal of Honor upon his return home. Wainwright liked San Antonio so much that he retired there after commanding the Fourth Army at Fort Sam Houston.

Third River Cornish Game Hens

These succulent little hens are wonderful for casual entertaining. They are delicious, and most of the work can be done before guests arrive. They are best cooked on a covered grill.

Yield: 4-6 servings

1 cup crumbled Chorizo or bulk sausage	Lightly brown Chorizo or bulk sausage and drain. Mix in mushrooms, olives and scallions or onions. Set aside. Wash thawed hens and pat dry. Place 1 tablespoon butter or margarine in body cavity of each hen. Stuff hens with equal amounts of sausage mixture and tie legs together. Brush hens lightly with olive oil and wrap in foil. Place breast side down on prepared charcoal grill, cover and cook for 25 minutes. Turn birds and cook for another 40 minutes. Open foil for the last 10 minutes to brown.

1 cup crumbled Chorizo or
bulk sausage
¾ cup sliced mushrooms
¾ cup sliced ripe olives
5-6 scallions or green onions,
chopped
4 Cornish game hens
4 tablespoons butter or
margarine
Olive oil

Lightly brown Chorizo or bulk sausage and drain. Mix in mushrooms, olives and scallions or onions. Set aside. Wash thawed hens and pat dry. Place 1 tablespoon butter or margarine in body cavity of each hen. Stuff hens with equal amounts of sausage mixture and tie legs together. Brush hens lightly with olive oil and wrap in foil. Place breast side down on prepared charcoal grill, cover and cook for 25 minutes. Turn birds and cook for another 40 minutes. Open foil for the last 10 minutes to brown.

Main Dishes

The Texas Declaration of Independence was adopted at Washington-on-the-Brazos in March 1836. Threatened by the advance of Santa Anna's troops following their victories at the Alamo and Goliad, the provisional capital became portable, moving to Harrisburg, Galveston and Velasco. A few months after the Texans' victory at San Jacinto, government officials moved to Columbia, making it officially the first capital of the Republic of Texas. It was here, in October 1836, that Sam Houston was inaugurated as Texas' first elected President. Two months later Houston moved the capital to the city that bears his name. In 1840 Waterloo was chosen as the capital's permanent site and the name of the town was changed to Austin.

Shrimp Scampi

Yield: 6 servings

2 pounds jumbo shrimp in shells
1 pound butter or margarine
2 tablespoons Worcestershire sauce
2 tablespoons lemon juice
1 teaspoon salt
1 clove garlic, minced
3-4 tablespoons black pepper

Place unpeeled shrimp in single layer in a large, flat pan. Combine remaining ingredients and pour over shrimp. Bake at 400° for 20-25 minutes, turning shrimp after 10 minutes. Baste with butter mixture every 5 minutes. Serve in the pan with fresh French bread to sop the butter mixture. (A damp finger towel for each guest will be appreciated.)

Variation: For Butterflied Shrimp Scampi, peel and devein shrimp, leaving tails attached. Slit each shrimp down the back almost all the way through, spread and place cut side down in a single layer in a shallow baking dish. Continue above recipe.

Main Dishes

Many Texas towns were founded by dreamers and schemers, but Port Arthur was the only city "ever located and built under direction from the spirit world . . . so recognized and acknowledged" according to founder Arthur Stillwell, who believed in hunches and supernatural creatures he called "Brownies." He had resolved to establish a rail and shipping terminus on the Texas coast; and he said that his "Brownies" told him to establish it on the site of an older colony, Aurora. Stillwell said he was able in dreams to envision Port Arthur exact in all detail, just as it was subsequently developed.

Crawfish Etouffée

East Texas cooking shows the influence of Creole and Cajun cooking. It is good eating.

Yield: 6 servings

½ cup butter or margarine
2 cups finely chopped onion
1 cup finely chopped celery
1 clove garlic, minced
½ cup Rotel Tomatoes, chopped in blender or food processor
1 cup water
1½ teaspoons salt
2 pounds cleaned crawfish tails, with fat
½ teaspoon red pepper
3 tablespoons flour
½ cup water

Melt butter in a large saucepan; add onion, celery and garlic and sauté until tender. Add tomatoes and simmer for 10 minutes. Add water and continue cooking over low heat for another 10 minutes. Add crawfish tails with fat and red pepper to mixture. Combine flour and water, stir until smooth and add to mixture. Cook and stir until crawfish are pink and tender. Serve over rice.

Main Dishes

Galveston—Texas' island city—was once the premier city in the state, larger and more sophisticated than Houston or Dallas. But the 1900 hurricane changed that, killing up to 6,000 people and destroying most of the city's buildings. Houston, which was protected by land, took the lead in the competition between the two cities. But Galveston didn't give up. It built a seawall and refashioned itself into a resort city. Lush and green year-round, Galveston has been called "the Oleander City" because of its colorful oleander bushes.

Texas Star Crabmeat Casserole

Yield: 6 servings

1 pound lump crabmeat
¼ cup lemon juice (juice of 3 lemons)
½ teaspoon salt
½ cup butter or margarine
2½ tablespoons all-purpose flour
1½ cups milk
½ teaspoon garlic salt
½ teaspoon celery salt
1 teaspoon parsley flakes
1 cup grated Cheddar cheese
2 tablespoons white wine (optional)
6 cups cooked wild rice or Uncle Ben's Wild Rice Mixture
1 6-ounce can sliced mushrooms, drained

Combine crabmeat, lemon juice and salt in a medium bowl and refrigerate while preparing sauce.

Melt butter or margarine in a medium saucepan. Add flour, stir and cook for about 1 minute. Add milk slowly, stirring constantly, and cook until sauce thickens. Add seasonings, cheese and wine (optional). Stir until cheese is melted and sauce is smooth. Drain crabmeat, add to sauce and heat until bubbly.

Layer cooked wild rice in bottom of a lightly oiled 2-quart casserole dish. Pour crabmeat and sauce over rice. Top with mushroom slices and bake at 350° for about 30 minutes or until lightly browned. Serve with a crisp green salad and crunchy rolls.

Deep-Fried Deviled Crab

This Galveston recipe calls for live blue crabs, which are not available in parts of Texas. However, it is also delicious made with fresh or frozen crabmeat and served in scallop shells.

Yield: 4 servings

12 **live blue crabs, boiled, cleaned and picked, (reserve 8-10 crab shells, washed and drained) or 1 pound fresh or frozen crabmeat**

1 **teaspoon salt**
Freshly ground black pepper

1 **cup finely chopped green onions, including tops**

1 **cup finely chopped celery**

6 **garlic cloves, minced**

2 **tablespoons finely chopped green bell pepper**

2 **tablespoons chopped parsley**

1 **small jalapeño pepper, seeded and diced (optional)**

2 **eggs**

½ **cup bread crumbs (reserve 2 tablespoons for topping)**

2 **tablespoons grated Italian cheese**

2 **cups vegetable oil**
Scallop shells if crab shells not available

Combine crabmeat, salt and a few grindings of black pepper in a large bowl. Add onions, celery, garlic, bell pepper, parsley and jalapeño (if desired). Stir in eggs, bread crumbs and cheese. Spoon mixture firmly into reserved crab shells, mounding slightly. Top with bread crumbs.

Heat oil until very hot but not smoking. Fry crabs, stuffed side down, until golden brown. Then turn shell side down and cook for another 2-3 minutes. Drain on paper towels.

If you do not have crab shells, form crabmeat mixture into 8-10 thick, firm patties rounded on top side. Press reserved bread crumbs on top. Lower carefully into hot oil with a slotted spoon so patties will stay intact. Turn when bottom side is browned. Drain on paper towels and place in oiled scallop shells to serve.

Tastes & Tales

VEGETABLES
AND SIDE DISHES

LBJ Birthplace

Vegetables and Side Dishes

The Hill Country near Comfort was settled by German colonists who pledged allegiance to the United States upon arrival in this country. When Texas voted to join the Confederacy at the start of the Civil War, they refused to break their oaths and take up arms against the Union. As a result, several of the counties near Comfort were declared in open rebellion by the Confederacy. In August 1862 more than 60 German men and boys tried to flee to Mexico, but they were pursued by Confederate soldiers and killed in two separate encounters. Today they are memorialized by an obelisk in Comfort that bears the inscription *Treue der Union* (Loyal to the Union), a reminder of one of the tragic episodes of the Civil War.

Horseshoe Mountain Ranch Pinto Beans

Jake Jacobson, owner of Horseshoe Mountain Ranch near Comfort, has perfected his recipe for pinto beans by tasting and testing until he found exactly the right combination of flavors in his version of a dish that is basic to Texas cooking. It's great for a cook-out or barbecue and only gets better when reheated.

Yield: 8-10 servings

1	pound pinto beans
1-2	quarts water
¼	pound ham hocks
1	tablespoon chili powder
1	tablespoon sugar
1	teaspoon black pepper
¼	teaspoon cumin
¼	teaspoon oregano
1	garlic clove, minced
1	large onion, chopped
1	teaspoon salt

Wash beans and place in a large pot or kettle. Add water and remaining ingredients (except salt, which should be added 30 minutes before beans are done). Cover and simmer for 5-6 hours. Check liquid level occasionally and add more water as needed.

Note: This recipe works especially well in a crockpot. (You will need 1 quart of water if using a crockpot; more if using a stove-top kettle.)

Vegetables and Side Dishes

Early German settlers moved into the Hill Country of Texas, founding such towns as New Braunfels, Fredericksburg, and Gruene. Most were hard-working farmers who raised an astonishing variety and quantity of vegetables and fruits on their small farms. Some would travel long distances to sell their produce in San Antonio—and even farther to sell to frontier military forts because the Army always paid in gold. Other early German settlers who stopped before getting to the Hill Country became Texas' first commercial gardeners, furnishing produce to Galveston, Indianola and Houston.

Gruene German Sauerkraut

Yield: 6 servings

1 quart sauerkraut
3 cups water
1 clove garlic
¼ teaspoon dill weed
¼ teaspoon cayenne pepper
2 pounds bratwurst or link sausage
1 teaspoon corn oil
1 large potato, grated

Drain and rinse sauerkraut. Combine with water, garlic, dill weed and cayenne pepper in a large saucepan and simmer for 1 hour. Brown bratwurst or link sausage in oil over medium heat. Stir sausage and drippings and grated potato into sauerkraut and simmer for 15 minutes or until potato has disintegrated and juice is thick and creamy. Stir frequently and, if necessary, add more water to prevent sticking.

Vegetables and Side Dishes

Austin's Scholz Garden, Texas' oldest beer garden and Austin's oldest business, was founded in 1862 by German immigrant August Scholz. For decades Scholz Garden has been the favorite watering hole for state lawmakers, earning it the nickname "Third House of the Texas Legislature." LBJ, many congressmen and a governor or six or seven have been patrons. The "Dearly Beloved Beer and Garden Party" in Texas writer Billy Lee Brammer's novel *The Gay Place* was patterned after Scholz Garden, which has recently been restored.

Scholz Garden Schnitzel Beans

A tasty vegetable dish zipped up with a bit of cayenne pepper. (You might want to start with a little of the cayenne and work up to your level of tolerance.)

Yield: 12 servings

2 pounds fresh green beans, cut in 1-inch pieces
8 slices bacon, diced
4 cups sliced onion
4 cups chopped tomato
1 teaspoon salt
1-3 teaspoons cayenne pepper (or less)
½ cup water

Place prepared beans in a large kettle. Fry bacon until crisp, drain and add to beans. Add onion, tomato, salt, cayenne pepper and water. Cook over low heat until beans are tender (about 10 minutes if beans are fresh).

Variation: Cooked sausage instead of bacon makes this into a savory one-dish meal. Cut the sausage into ½-inch slices before adding to vegetables.

Vegetables and Side Dishes

The history of the Texas Navy reflects the chaotic nature of the Republic which created it in 1835. Privateers formed the first Texas Navy. The new Republic bought 4 ships and lost them all within a year. Texas' third president, Mirabeau Lamar, believed in a strong navy; but when Sam Houston was re-elected to succeed him, one of his ways of trying to balance the budget was to cut navy appropriations. By 1840 the Texas Navy had 6 new ships, which it promptly rented to the Republic of Yucatan. In 1843 Houston declared the Texas Navy to be "pirates", then later tried to sell the ships at auction. In June 1846 the Texas Navy was absorbed by the United States Navy.

Stewed Tomato Casserole

Yield: 6 servings

6 slices bacon, chopped
½ cup chopped onion
4 cups canned tomatoes
2 teaspoons brown sugar
1 teaspoon salt
½ teaspoon oregano
½ teaspoon black pepper
4 slices bread (French-type preferably)
2 tablespoons butter or margarine
Grated Parmesan cheese

Fry bacon in a large skillet until partially cooked. Add onion and sauté until transparent. Stir in tomatoes, brown sugar and seasonings. Tear bread into small pieces and add to mixture. Pour into a 1½-quart buttered casserole dish. Dot with butter and sprinkle with Parmesan cheese. Bake at 350° for about 30 minutes or until bubbly.

Vegetables and Side Dishes

Experts say Caddo Lake was formed by a log jam in the Red River, but Caddo Indian legend holds that there was once a great village there. A Caddo chief was warned by the Great Spirit to take his people to higher ground or see them killed by earthquake and flood, but he paid no heed and took his warriors hunting. When they returned, the village was gone and a lake had formed in its place. The Caddos thereafter referred to the region as "the trembling ground" after the earthquake that they said formed the lake.

Tomatoes Rockefeller

If I were to rank this recipe by stars, it would rate four of them. It is delicious, and can be made ahead.

Yield: 8 servings

6 large tomatoes, peeled
3 10-ounce packages frozen chopped spinach
6 green onions, chopped
½ teaspoon minced garlic
6 eggs, beaten
½ cup melted margarine
½ teaspoon Worcestershire sauce
¼ teaspoon Tabasco
1 teaspoon salt
½ teaspoon oregano
½ teaspoon thyme
½ teaspoon lemon pepper
1 cup bread crumbs (reserve ¼ cup for topping)
½ cup grated Mozzarella cheese (reserve ¼ cup for topping)

Slice each tomato into 3 thick slices. Arrange in a single layer in bottom of a 9x12-inch oiled baking dish. Cook spinach until completely thawed. Drain in a sieve, pressing to remove some of the liquid. Combine remaining ingredients except for reserved bread crumbs and cheese. Mound a large spoonful of spinach mixture on top of each slice of tomato. Top with reserved cheese and bread crumbs. Bake at 350° for 20-25 minutes.

Vegetables and Side Dishes

The first shot of the Texas Revolution was fired on October 2, 1835, by Texians at Gonzales. Mexican soldiers had been sent to fetch a small cannon which the Texians refused to give up. The determined Texians displayed a white cotton flag designed with a single star at the top and inscribed with the message "Come and Take It". Noah Smithwick, who fought at Gonzales, wrote, "I cannot remember that there was any distinct understanding as to the position we were to assume toward Mexico. Some were for Independence, some for the Constitution of 1824, and some for anything, just so it was a row. But we were all ready to fight." And fight they did, defeating the Mexican force with squirrel guns, hunting knives, and the little cannon the Mexicans came to get.

Spinach-Stuffed Artichokes

Yield: 4-6 servings

2 14-ounce cans artichoke bottoms (found in gourmet shops)
3 tablespoons butter or margarine
¼ cup chopped onion
1 10-ounce package frozen chopped spinach, thawed and drained
¼ cup sour cream
2 tablespoons grated fresh Parmesan cheese
Salt and pepper

Drain artichoke bottoms and place in a 9x9-inch glass baking dish. Melt butter or margarine in a medium skillet and sauté onion until glossy. Add spinach, sour cream and 1½ tablespoons Parmesan cheese. Mix gently. Add salt and pepper to taste. Mound a rounded tablespoon of spinach mixture on top of each artichoke and sprinkle with remaining cheese. Cover with foil and bake at 350° for 30 minutes.

Gail Borden of condensed milk fame also enjoyed "doctoring". His philosophy? "It is no use to be a doctor unless you put on the airs of one. Nine times out of ten sickness is caused by overeating or eating unwholesome food, but a patient gets angry if you tell him so; you must humor him. This I do by taking calomel (a purgative), dividing it into infinitesimal parts, adding sufficient starch to make little pellets, then glaze them over with sugar. In prescribing for a patient, I caution him about his diet and warn him that the pills have calomel in them. Well, the result is that he abstains from hurtful articles of food, which is all he needs to do anyway."

Stuffed Mushrooms

Surround a rib roast or tenderloin with these delicious treats, tuck in some parsley or leaf lettuce and serve to your favorite people.

Yield: 4 servings

12 large mushrooms
¼ cup butter or margarine
½ cup finely chopped onion
2 cloves garlic, minced
½ teaspoon salt
¼ teaspoon oregano
½ cup dry bread crumbs
   Grated Parmesan cheese
3 tablespoons melted butter or margarine

Clean mushrooms with a damp cloth. Remove stems and chop into very small pieces. Heat butter or margarine in a large skillet; add chopped mushroom stems, onion and garlic. Sauté until onion is tender. Add seasonings and bread crumbs. Spoon stuffing mixture into mushroom caps. Sprinkle with Parmesan cheese. Pour melted butter or margarine in an 8x8-inch glass baking dish. Add mushrooms, turning to coat bottoms and sides. Bake at 350° for 20 minutes.

Carrot Ring

This is especially good to use when you are serving buffet style. It's attractive, tasty and easy to serve.

Yield: 8 servings

¼ cup fine bread crumbs
1 scant cup shortening
¼ cup brown sugar
1 egg, beaten
1½ cups grated carrots
1¼ cups flour
1 teaspoon salt
1 teaspoon baking powder
1 teaspoon soda
2 teaspoons lemon juice
1 tablespoon cold water

Oil a 1½-quart ring mold and sprinkle with half the bread crumbs. Mix remaining ingredients in order given and pour into mold. Scatter remaining bread crumbs over top of batter. Bake at 350° for 35-40 minutes or until carrot ring begins to pull away from sides of mold. Allow carrot ring to rest for 5 minutes. Loosen from mold by running a knife around sides and carefully unmold onto a serving plate.

Mushroom Sauce:

1 10¾-ounce can cream of mushroom soup
1 4-ounce can sliced mushrooms
1 teaspoon Kitchen Bouquet flavoring
½ teaspoon seasoned salt
Salt and pepper to taste

Combine sauce ingredients in a medium saucepan and bring to a boil. Serve in a glass that fits center of ring mold. Let your guests ladle sauce on top of carrot ring wedges.

Sweet-and-Sour Glazed Carrots

Yield: 4 servings

4 large carrots, peeled and
 thickly sliced
2 cups water
3 tablespoons brown sugar
1 tablespoon butter
1 tablespoon parsley flakes
½ teaspoon seasoned salt
1½ tablespoons red wine
 vinegar
2 teaspoons cornstarch

Bring carrots to a boil in a medium saucepan. Add brown sugar, cover and cook until tender. Drain off half of the water and return carrots to low heat. Add butter, parsley flakes, seasoned salt and vinegar. Dissolve cornstarch in a small portion of the carrot sauce. Combine with carrots and heat until sauce begins to thicken.

Carrot and Zucchini Julienne

Fresh tasting and pretty. Choose the long, firm zucchini—they are usually crisper and have fewer seeds.

Yield: 6 servings

2 medium zucchini, unpeeled
4 medium carrots, scraped
¼ cup melted butter or
 margarine
1 teaspoon minced chives
½ teaspoon salt
¼ teaspoon white pepper

Cut zucchini and carrots lengthwise into slices ¼-inch thick. Stack slices and cut into ¼-inch strips about 3 inches long. (Or use julienne blade on your food processor.) Layer carrots on bottom of steamer basket, with zucchini on top. Place steamer basket over 3 cups of boiling water and cook for 5-7 minutes or until tender. Combine butter or margarine, chives, salt and pepper and toss gently with vegetables in a warm serving dish.

Scalloped Corn

What could be easier than this great-tasting corn casserole.

Yield: 6 servings

2 17-ounce cans whole-kernel corn
2 eggs, beaten
1 cup cracker crumbs
¼ teaspoon salt
¼ teaspoon pepper
½ cup butter or margarine
2 tablespoons chopped onion
1 cup milk

Drain corn and place in a large mixing bowl. Add eggs, cracker crumbs, salt and pepper. Melt butter or margarine in a small saucepan, add onions and cook until transparent. Add milk and heat until warm. Stir into corn mixture. Pour into greased 1½-quart casserole dish. Bake at 350° for 30 minutes or until center of casserole is firm.

Corn Casserole

A modern version of a favorite Texas corn recipe.

Yield: 8 servings

1 17-ounce can whole-kernel corn
1 17-ounce can cream-style corn
1 cup sour cream
½ cup melted margarine
1 8½-ounce package Jiffy Corn Muffin Mix

Combine ingredients, mix thoroughly and pour into a 2-quart casserole dish. Bake in a 300° oven for 1 hour and 40 minutes.

Variation: Add 2 tablespoons finely chopped onion and 2 tablespoons finely chopped red or green bell pepper.

Vegetables and Side Dishes

It took people as fearless and tough as the W.T. Buntin family, the first settlers of Wichita County, to tame the Texas frontier. Testified an old playmate of the Buntin kids:

"They went barefooted summer and winter, and wore crude, homemade garments fashioned by their mother from tarpaulins which their father brought back from Fort Sill. I remember going hunting with one of the boys. He insisted we go barehanded. We climbed into a mesquite tree and down in the brush below us was a big bobcat. The Buntin boy cut a branch from the tree and poked down into the brush to rout the bobcat. Then he jumped on top of the 'cat and subdued him with his bare hands."

Temple Stuffed Squash

Yield: 4-6 servings

6 medium yellow squash
2 hard-boiled eggs
3-4 tablespoons minced onion
1 tablespoon sugar
4 tablespoons melted butter
Salt and pepper to taste
¾ cup finely crushed saltine crackers

Cook squash in boiling, salted water until tender. Remove from water and cool. Discard stem ends and slice lengthwise. Scoop pulp from center of each squash and place in a medium mixing bowl. Set squash shells aside. Mash or sieve hard-boiled eggs and add to squash. Combine onion, sugar, butter, salt and pepper with squash mixture. Add cracker crumbs until mixture is not soupy. Pile squash mixture into shells and bake at 350° for 20-25 minutes or until lightly browned.

Vegetables and Side Dishes

The first steamboat to reach Houston arrived in January 1837 after taking 3 days to journey the 16 miles from Harrisburg. The crew of the steamboat, the Laura M., had to hack their way through the dense, overhanging vegetation; and the cook went overboard at a sudden lurch, never to be found. Despite the Allen brothers' enthusiastic promotion throughout the United States, Houston was still so insignificant that the skipper of the Laura M. went 3 miles past the stakes marking the trail from Buffalo Bayou to town and had to back up.

Wooden Star Squash

Even 6-year-olds who think they don't like vegetables love this. It is really good.

Yield: 8 servings

8-10 medium yellow squash, sliced
½ cup chopped onion
2 envelopes Lipton Cup-a-Soup Cream of Chicken dry soup mix
1 cup boiling water
1 teaspoon sugar
1 teaspoon margarine
1 cup sour cream
1½ cups Pepperidge Farm Cornbread Stuffing

Cook squash and onion in small amount of boiling, salted water until barely tender (about 10 minutes). Drain well. Put contents of both envelopes of cream of chicken soup mix in a large bowl, add boiling water and stir. Add squash, onion, sugar, margarine and sour cream and mix gently. Spread half the cornbread stuffing in the bottom of a 9x13-inch baking pan and pour squash mixture over it. Top with remaining stuffing and bake in a 350° oven for 35 minutes or until browned.

Vegetables and Side Dishes

On July 4, 1865, the Confederate General Joseph O. Shelby and his unsurrendered division of Missouri Cavalry crossed the Rio Grande into Mexico at Eagle Pass. Before crossing that morning, the 500 veterans gathered around their battle flag while four colonels weighted it with stones and reverently lowered it into the river's muddy waters. Shelby then tore the plume from his hat and cast it behind him into the river. Their flag was the last to fly over an unsurrendered force, and that spot is often referred to as the grave of the Confederacy.

Bourbon Sweet Potatoes

Brought from Kentucky by Edith Keller, this recipe quickly became a favorite of her Texas friends.

Yield: 8 servings

4 pounds (4-6) sweet potatoes (canned ones may be used)
¼-½ cup bourbon
1 teaspoon salt
½ cup butter or margarine
¼ cup light brown sugar
¼ teaspoon ground cloves
⅓ cup orange juice
⅓ cup chopped pecans
1 cup miniature marshmallows

Cook potatoes in salted water until tender. Drain, cool slightly and peel. (Or use canned ones.) Mash potatoes, add remaining ingredients except for nuts and marshmallows and beat until smooth. Stir in nuts and spoon into a large buttered baking dish. Bake at 350° for 40 minutes. Top with marshmallows and bake until golden brown.

Variation: For a different topping, combine ½ cup chopped pecans, ½ cup brown sugar, ½ cup coconut and 3 teaspoons butter and sprinkle over top of sweet potatoes. Bake until coconut begins to brown.

Juneteenth is a uniquely Texas summer holiday. Although the Civil War had been over for several months, it wasn't until June 19, 1865, that General Gordon Granger finally landed at Galveston to repossess Texas for the Union. He made official the rumor that "all slaves are free" and joyous former slaves immediately made June 19th their Emancipation Day. Texas is the only state that observes the day as a legal holiday, and each year Blacks gather for the traditional Juneteenth parades and picnics in jubilant commemoration.

Cheese-Stuffed Baked Potatoes

Yield: 6 servings

6 medium baking potatoes
Vegetable oil
¼ cup butter or margarine
½ cup milk
2 tablespoons finely chopped green onion
1 cup shredded Cheddar cheese
½ teaspoon salt
¼ teaspoon pepper
3 slices bacon, cooked and crumbled

Scrub potatoes with a vegetable brush, dry and rub skins with oil. Prick potatoes 2 or 3 times with a fork. Bake at 400° for 1 hour or until soft. Remove from oven and let cool slightly.

Cut a slice from top of each potato. Carefully scoop out pulp, leaving potato skin shell intact. Mash potato pulp, add butter and milk and beat until smooth. Stir in onion, cheese, salt and pepper. Spoon mixture into potato shells, sprinkle with crumbled bacon and bake at 350° for 20 minutes.

Note: If you want to freeze stuffed potatoes, leave bacon off until ready to heat. Allow to thaw before heating.

Vegetables and Side Dishes

Some of our greatest inventions have resulted from lucky accidents; and in such a way was agriculture introduced to parts of the Panhandle. About 1900 in Colorado City the accidental sprouting of an Irish potato in front of the bank led to the decision that farming might pay off, which it has. Likewise, cotton production around Amarillo began after the discovery that "woolly beans"—cotton seeds in which a shipment of eggs had been packed—would grow.

Cheesy Potatoes

This easy and delicious potato casserole is one of those no-fail recipes that can be put together ahead of time and baked at dinner time.

Yield: 6-8 servings

1 2-pound bag frozen hash brown potatoes, thawed
1 medium onion, chopped
  Salt and pepper to taste
1¼ sticks corn oil margarine
1 10¾-ounce can undiluted cream of chicken soup
8 ounces American process cheese
1 8-ounce carton sour cream
1½ cups crushed corn flakes

Spread hash browns in a 9x13-inch baking dish. Sprinkle with onion, salt and pepper. Melt margarine and pour half over potatoes. (Reserve remaining margarine for topping.) Heat soup and cheese in a medium saucepan, stirring until cheese is melted. Mix in sour cream and pour mixture over potatoes.

Combine crushed corn flakes and reserved margarine and sprinkle evenly over top of sour cream and cheese mixture. Bake at 350° for 1 hour.

Tip: To prolong freshness of cheese after original wrapping is removed, apply a thin film of margarine or oil to any exposed area and rewrap carefully in plastic wrap.

Vegetables and Side Dishes

When the winds begin to blow cold up North, thousands of Winter Texans migrate to the Lower Rio Grande Valley to enjoy the warm sun, the South Padre Island beaches, the luscious tree-ripened citrus fruits and the friendships made during previous visits to the area. For those that are bird lovers, the Santa Ana National Wildlife Refuge teems with innumerable species including tropical birds not found elsewhere in the U. S. Visitors to the area also enjoy the Gladys Porter Zoo in Brownsville which features endangered species from throughout the world. The one-way glass mirrors and natural settings found at the zoo make it a very special place to visit.

Rio Grande Onion Pie

Yield: 7 servings

1 cup saltine crackers, finely crushed
6 tablespoons melted butter
3 cups onion, thinly sliced
3 eggs, lightly beaten
¾ cup light cream
1 teaspoon salt
Dash of pepper
⅔ cup shredded sharp Cheddar cheese

Combine cracker crumbs and 4 tablespoons butter in a 9-inch pie plate; mix with a fork. Spread crumbs and press firmly to form crust.

Place remaining butter in a skillet. Add onion and cook over medium heat, stirring occasionaly until tender. Transfer to pie shell. Combine eggs, cream, salt and pepper in a small saucepan. Stir over medium heat until hot but not boiling. Pour over onion. Top with cheese, and bake at 350° for 30 minutes.

The incredible story of the huge oil discovery near Kilgore is told at the East Texas Oil Museum at Kilgore College. It is "a tribute to the independent oil producers and wildcatters, to the men and women who dared to dream." The quiet rural life in Kilgore was changed forever when "Dad" Joiner, a 70-year-old wildcatter, brought in a gusher on the Daisy Bradford farm in October 1930. At one time there were more than 1,000 wells in downtown Kilgore, and a large number of them were festooned with tree lights during the Christmas season.

French-Fried Onion Rings

Onion rings fried in peanut oil taste better than those fried in shortening and they have less cholesterol.

Yield: 6-8 servings

6 medium Spanish onions, thinly sliced
1 cup milk
1 cup buttermilk
1 egg, beaten
1 cup all-purpose flour
2-3 cups peanut oil
Salt to taste

Separate onion slices into rings. Combine milk, buttermilk and egg in a medium mixing bowl. Add onion rings and refrigerate for 30 minutes. Spread flour on a plate. Heat oil to 375° in a medium saucepan or deep-fat fryer. Remove onion rings from milk mixture and dip one at a time into flour. Fry in hot oil until golden brown. Cook no more that 8-10 rings at one time to prevent oil from cooling below 375°. Remove from oil, drain on paper towels and sprinkle with salt.

Tip: Some types of onions work better than others for certain uses. Spanish onions are best for frying and are attractive and good in salads. Yellow onions are good for stuffing and for French-frying. The little white boiling onions are great in stews or for creaming. The mild sweet onions, especially the Texas 1015 (named for date planted) are tops for salads and sandwiches. For the past two years the Texas 1015 has won the National Sweet Onion Challenge, beating out Georgia's fabled Vidalia.

Vegetables and Side Dishes

Dr. Arthur Scott of Temple saw the need for better medical facilities in the area while he was still a doctor for the Santa Fe Railroad. Knowing he would need help, he began looking for a partner. He interviewed Dr. Raleigh R. Scott and was so impressed that he hired him on the spot. Together these two idealistic young frontier doctors started the Temple Sanitorium. They bought a house and converted it into an 8-bed hospital. As their reputations grew, so did Scott & White; and by 1963, when the new hospital was built, the complex had 28 buildings. It is now one of the largest multi-specialty clinics in the nation and schedules more than 700,000 outpatient visits per year.

Green Chile Quiche

From Jan Temple, one of the hard-working volunteers at Scott & White Hospital.

Yield: 6 servings

½ pound ground beef
¼ cup chopped onion
1 9-inch pastry shell
1 4-ounce can chopped green chiles, drained
2 cups shredded Monterey Jack cheese
3 eggs, beaten
1 cup milk
¼ teaspoon salt
   Dash of garlic powder

Cook ground beef and onion in a medium skillet until lightly browned. Spread in pastry shell and top with green chiles and cheese. Combine last 4 ingredients and pour over cheese and meat. Bake at 375° for 40 minutes or until set.

Tip: *Shredding cheese is much easier if cheese is partially frozen. One-half pound cheese yields about 2 cups shredded cheese.*

Rice was first grown in Texas around Beaumont soon after the town's founding in 1837. The first harvests were meager but yielded enough to demonstrate that the crop could be grown profitably. It was sometimes called "providence rice" because farmers depended on nature to provide the critical moisture. Low-lying fields were plowed and the rice seed were broadcast by hand, then harrowed into the ground. After levees were built, everyone prayed for rain. Large-scale production of rice did not begin until irrigation pumps were introduced well after the Civil War.

Providence Rice and Green Chiles

This good casserole is a wonderful way to use left-over rice.

Yield: 6 servings

½ cup sour cream
¼ cup milk
4 cups cooked rice
1 4-ounce can chopped green chiles, drained
½ teaspoon salt
¼ teaspoon pepper
1 cup grated American cheese

Blend sour cream and milk together in a medium bowl. Add rice and mix. Add chiles, salt and pepper. Spoon into a 2-quart greased casserole dish. Sprinkle cheese over top. Bake at 350° for 25-30 minutes.

Tip: To keep rice from becoming discolored or sticky, add ½ teaspoon vinegar to the cooking water.

Hot Grits

Yield: 10 servings

1½ cups quick-cooking grits
6 cups water
3 eggs, slightly beaten
2 teaspoons seasoned salt
1 teaspoon Tabasco
1 tablespoon Worcestershire sauce
1 pound grated American cheese
½ cup margarine
4 ounces chopped green chilies

Slowly stir grits into boiling water and cook for 2½ minutes. Remove from heat. Add remaining ingredients to grits and pour into a lightly greased 3-quart baking dish. Bake at 325° for 1 hour. This freezes well.

Chile Relleno Pie

Yield: 8 servings

8 ounces chopped green chiles
1 pound grated Monterey Jack cheese
4 eggs, beaten
4 cups milk
1 cup flour
2 teaspoons salt
Paprika

Line an oiled 9x13-inch baking pan with chiles. Sprinkle cheese over chiles. Combine eggs, milk, flour and salt and beat until frothy. Pour over chiles and cheese. Sprinkle paprika on top and bake at 350° for 10 minutes. Lower heat to 325° and continue baking for 50 minutes or until knife inserted in center comes out clean.

Tastes & Tales

SWEETS
AND TREATS

Big Bend Country

Pofirio Salinas was Texas' most famous painter of bluebonnets. Born in Bastrop in 1910, he never had any formal art training. After World War II he became Texas' most popular artist, famous for his Central and West Texas landscapes, his bluebonnets, cactus, and huisache. Salinas' paintings, which have been collected by J. Frank Dobie, Lyndon B. Johnson, Sam Rayburn and John Connally, hang in the national capitols of both the U.S. and Mexico.

Marble Falls Favorite Chocolate Cake

The chocolate syrup gives this cake a wonderful velvety texture. This recipe comes from the area where the bluebonnets put on their most spectacular show each spring.

Yield: 12 servings

½ cup butter or margarine
1 cup sugar
4 eggs
1 cup all-purpose flour
1 teaspoon baking powder
1 16-ounce can Hershey's chocolate syrup
1 cup chopped pecans
1 teaspoon vanilla

Cream butter or margarine and sugar together and beat until light. Add eggs one at a time, beating thoroughly after each addition. Add sifted dry ingredients and chocolate syrup alternately, blending well.

Pour batter into a well-greased and floured tube or bundt pan. Bake in a preheated 350° oven for 45 minutes. Spread with Lemon Glaze when almost cool.

Lemon Glaze:

3 teaspoons lemon juice
½ teaspoon grated lemon rind
½ cup sifted powdered sugar

Combine ingredients and spoon over top of cake.

The freewheeling, range-riding, gun-toting cowboy of the late 1900's is part of the Texas legend. His code of behavior meant that he shared his food with strangers without asking questions, he was polite to the ladies and he hung any man caught stealing a horse. And although his food was monotonous, not a pat of butter or a drop of milk could be found on early ranch tables because Texas cowboys considered milking a cow beneath their dignity.

Button's Brandy Cake

This elegant dessert will have your guests purring with delight.

Yield: 8-10 servings

1 cup soft butter
2 cups confectioners sugar
5 egg yolks
½ cup brandy
1 cup toasted slivered almonds
1 large angel food cake

Blend butter and confectioners sugar and beat until fluffy. Add egg yolks one at a time, beating well after each addition. Add brandy and almonds and mix well. Line a 2-quart mixing bowl with waxed paper. Slice ½-inch from top of angel food cake and place on bottom of bowl. Spoon a layer of brandy mixture over cake. Slice remaining cake into 3 equal layers and alternate layers of cake and brandy mixture. Chill overnight. Turn molded cake out on your prettiest cake plate and frost.

Frosting:
1 pint whipping cream
2 tablespoons confectioners sugar
¼ cup brandy
1 teaspoon vanilla

Whip cream until stiff. Add confectioners sugar, brandy and vanilla and mix well. Frost cake with whipped cream mixture and garnish with fresh mint leaves and strawberries.

Sweets and Treats

The hamlet of Knickerbocker near San Angelo is most famous as the birthplace of the outlaw Tom "Black Jack" Ketchum. As leader of The Wild Bunch, Black Jack and his brother Sam held up trains, stores and post offices. No one talks much about the Ketchums at the annual Knickerbocker Homecoming and Picnic, where some of Texas' best barbequed goat is served.

Lemon Buttermilk Cake

Yield: 14 servings

2½ cups sugar
1½ cups shortening
4 large eggs, at room temperature
3½ cups all-purpose flour
½ teaspoon soda
1 teaspoon salt
1 cup buttermilk
1 tablespoon water
1 tablespoon lemon extract

Cream sugar and shortening. Add eggs, one at a time, beating after each addition. Sift flour, soda, and salt together. Add to creamed mixture alternately with buttermilk and water. Mix in lemon extract.

Pour into a greased and floured tube pan. Bake at 350° for 1 hour and 15 minutes. Leave in pan and spread with Lemon Glaze while still hot.

Lemon Glaze:

Juice of 2 lemons
1 cup sugar
2 tablespoons hot water

Combine ingredients in a small saucepan. Boil for 4 minutes over medium heat. Pour over cake while still hot. Wait 15 minutes before removing cake from pan.

The Sam Houston Memorial Museum in Huntsville gives visitors a glimpse of the man who led the fight for Texas' independence and later became President of the Republic of Texas, U.S. Senator from Texas and Governor of Texas. The museum complex includes the Exhibit Hall with its collection of Houston memorabilia; the Woodland Home, which was built by Sam Houston in 1848 and where four of his eight children were born; and the Steamboat House, where he lived from the time he resigned as Governor in 1861 until his death in 1863. The Museum is a non-profit activity associated with Sam Houston State University.

Alamo Lemon Jelly Cake

This is the type of dessert Sam Houston liked best. The recipe is reprinted from the Sam Houston Memorial Museum Quarterly with their permission.

Yield: 12-16 servings

¾ cup butter, margarine or shortening
2 cups sugar
6 eggs
3 cups sifted all-purpose flour
3 teaspoons baking powder
¼ teaspoon salt
½ teaspoon lemon extract
1½ cups milk

Lemon Filling:

2 eggs
1 cup sugar
1 tablespoon butter or margarine
Rind of 1 lemon, grated
Juice of 2 lemons (¼ cup)

Preheat oven to 375°. Grease and flour three 8-inch cake pans. Work butter, margarine or shortening in mixing bowl until soft, then add sugar gradually and continue working mixture until it is smooth and creamy. Separate egg yolks from whites, beating yolks one at a time into creamed mixture. Beat hard after each addition.

Sift flour, baking powder and salt together several times. Stir lemon extract into milk and mix liquid alternately with dry ingredients into creamed mixture. Beat egg whites until they hold a point and fold into batter until whites are blended in. Pour into cake pans and bake for 35 minutes or until cake pulls away from sides of pans. Remove from pans and let cool. Spread a thin coating of lemon filling between each layer and over the top.

Beat eggs slightly in a saucepan. Stir in sugar, butter or margarine, lemon rind and juice and cook over low heat, stirring constantly, until filling is thick enough to coat a spoon (10-15 minutes). Cool.

Waco was originally an Indian village located beside a group of gushing springs. In Waco Indian legend, the Great Spirit led the Wacos to the fertile Brazos Valley, promising that they would flourish as long as they drank from the springs. But about 1830 raiding Cherokees drove the Wacos away. In 1855 they were forced to go to a reservation, but only after being allowed to drink from their revered springs one last time.

Opal's Peanut Butter Cake

This Waco recipe came highly recommended by friends of the cook. It is destined to become a favorite of the peanut butter lovers at your house.

Yield: 12 servings

2 cups sifted all-purpose flour
1½ cups sugar
2½ teaspoons baking powder
¾ teaspoon salt
½ cup shortening, at room temperature
⅔ cup milk
2 eggs
¼ cup milk
2 tablespoons peanut butter

Sift dry ingredients together in a large bowl. Add shortening and milk; beat for 2 minutes at medium speed with an electric mixer. Add eggs and milk; beat for 1 minute. Add peanut butter to batter; beat at low speed until thoroughly mixed.

Grease two 8-inch cake pans, line with waxed paper; grease paper, sprinkle with flour and shake out excess. Divide batter equally between the pans and bake at 350° for 25-30 minutes.

For icing, spread with your favorite peanut butter while cake is warm or use Chocolate-Peanut Butter Frosting.

Chocolate-Peanut Butter Frosting:

1 6-ounce package chocolate chips
½ cup butter or margarine
½-¾ cup sifted confectioners sugar
1¼ cups peanut butter

Melt chocolate chips and butter in a double boiler. Add confectioners sugar and peanut butter and beat until smooth. Chill for about 15 minutes or until frosting is of spreading consistency.

The Mission San Jose, San Antonio's "Queen of Missions," has been described as the most elegant Spanish mission building in North America. Built sometime around 1770, its most famous feature is the large, beautifully sculptured "Rose Window" on the sacristy wall. A stone carver, Pedro Huizar, has been given credit for the window. Legend says a broken heart was his inspiration after his beautiful sweetheart, Rosa, died in a shipwreck as she sailed from Spain to New Spain to marry him. Recent research says the story is probably not true, but the romantic legend lingers on.

Mexican Wedding Cake

A luscious, moist cake that is easy to make.

Yield: 12-14 servings

2 **cups sugar**
2 **cups all-purpose flour**
1 **teaspoon soda**
1 **teaspoon vanilla**
1 **20-ounce can crushed pineapple (with juice)**
½ **cup chopped pecans**

Combine all ingredients in a large bowl. Pour into a 9x12-inch greased and floured baking pan and bake at 350° for 30 minutes. (Bake an additional 10 minutes if using a glass baking dish.)

Frosting:
½ **cup softened margarine**
1 **8-ounce package cream cheese**
¾ **cup granulated sugar**
½ **cup chopped pecans**
1 **teaspoon vanilla**

Beat margarine, cream cheese and sugar until fluffy. Add pecans and vanilla and mix well. Spread frosting while cake is slightly warm.

Sweets and Treats

Jesse Chisholm died in 1868 without an inkling of the fame his name would attain. The old Indian trader worked out a 220-mile trail from central Oklahoma to Wichita, Kansas, in 1865, and his Anglo and Indian friends quickly began travelling this route. Soon it became part of a much longer trail system stretching from Brownsville to Abilene, Kansas. Millions of Texas cattle were driven along its route; and by the early 1870's the whole trail had become known as the Chisholm Trail, honoring the man whose tombstone reads, "No man ever left his home cold or hungry."

Texas Sausage Cake

A rich, moist spice cake. No, you don't taste the sausage.

Yield: 12 servings

3 cups packed brown sugar
1 pound lean bulk sausage (mildly seasoned)
1 egg, beaten
3¼ cups sifted all-purpose flour
2 teaspoons soda
3 teaspoons baking powder
1 teaspoon nutmeg
2 teaspoons cinnamon
¼ teaspoon salt
1 cup strong black coffee
2 teaspoons vanilla
½ cup raisins, dredged in flour
1 cup chopped pecans

Combine brown sugar and sausage in a large mixing bowl. Add egg and mix well. Sift dry ingredients together and add to sausage mixture alternately with coffee. Stir in vanilla. Add flour-coated raisins and pecans and stir until thoroughly combined.

Pour into a well-greased tube pan and bake at 350° for 1¼ hours. Cool for 20 minutes before removing from pan. Spread with Confectioners Glaze.

Confectioners Glaze:

2 tablespoons milk
½-¾ cup sifted confectioners sugar

Mix milk with ½ cup confectioners sugar (more if needed) until mixture is of a thin, spreading consistency. Spoon over top of cake.

Wild mustang grape wine, an old Texas standard, is hard to find these days. It was made by immigrants from southern Germany, where wine predominated over beer. The Germans had to modify their European processes, especially in adding lots of sugar to the very sour juice after first fermentation. Most of the vintners were tight-lipped about their processes, and their secrets died with them. The Star of Fredericksburg Winery made wine from native grapes and berries until the 1940's. A few old Germans still make mustang grape wine—strong, sweet, and with a delayed punch.

Fredericksburg Peach Kuchen

Yield: 12 servings

½ cup softened butter or margarine
1 18-ounce package yellow-cake mix
4-5 ripe peaches, thinly sliced
½ cup sugar
1 teaspoon cinnamon
1 cup commercial sour cream
1 egg, slightly beaten

Cut butter into cake mix until mixture resembles a coarse meal. Press into bottom of a greased 9x13-inch baking dish. Bake at 350° for 10 minutes. Layer sliced peaches on baked crust.

Combine sugar and cinnamon and sprinkle over peaches. Mix sour cream and egg and spread evenly on top of peaches. Bake for 20-25 minutes or until cake begins to brown around the edges.

Texas Chocolate Sheet Cake

A classic chocolate cake that's about as good as a cake can be.

Yield: 14-16 servings

2 cups sugar
2 cups all-purpose flour
1 teaspoon soda
1 teaspoon cinnamon
1 cup water
½ cup butter or margarine
½ cup vegetable oil
¼ cup cocoa
½ cup buttermilk
2 eggs, slightly beaten
1 teaspoon vanilla

Sift sugar, flour, soda and cinnamon together into a large mixing bowl. Set aside. Combine water, butter or margarine, oil and cocoa in a small saucepan and bring to a boil, stirring constantly. (Watch carefully so mixture does not scorch.) Pour over dry ingredients and mix well. Combine buttermilk, eggs and vanilla and stir into chocolate batter. Pour batter into a greased and floured 9x13-inch cake pan. Bake at 375° for 25 minutes (slightly longer if using a glass pan). Start making Chocolate Mocha Frosting about 5 minutes before cake is done.

Chocolate-Mocha Frosting

Yield: For a 9x13-inch cake

6 tablespoons butter
or margarine
¼ cup cocoa
⅓ cup strong coffee (⅓ cup milk may be substituted)
3 cups confectioners sugar
1 teaspoon vanilla
1 cup chopped pecans

Combine butter or margarine, cocoa and coffee (or milk) in a small saucepan and bring to a boil, stirring constantly. Stir in confectioners sugar gradually. Add vanilla and pecans. Mix and spread on the hot cake while it is still in the pan.

Old-Fashioned Prune Cake

The blend of spices and prunes makes an unusually good cake. It can be baked in a bundt pan and served unfrosted or made as a layer cake with Boiled Caramel Frosting.

Yield: 14 servings

½ cup butter or margarine
1 cup brown sugar
2 eggs
1 cup chopped cooked prunes
2 cups flour
1 teaspoon soda
1 teaspoon baking powder
1 teaspoon ground cinnamon
1 teaspoon ground cloves
1 teaspoon allspice
1 cup buttermilk
1 cup rolled oats

Cream butter or margarine with brown sugar until light and fluffy. Add eggs and prunes. Combine flour, soda, baking powder and spices and sift together. Add to creamed mixture alternately with buttermilk to facilitate even mixing. Add oats and mix thoroughly. Bake in two oiled 9-inch layer cake pans at 375° for 25 minutes. Or bake in an oiled bundt pan for 40-45 minutes. Spread with Boiled Caramel Frosting.

Boiled Caramel Frosting

An old-fashioned frosting that takes careful watching and beating; but when you taste the flavor, you'll know it's worth the effort.

Yield: Enough for a 2-layer cake

1½ cups firmly packed brown sugar
1½ cups granulated sugar
1½ cups milk
2 teaspoons butter

Combine sugars and milk and bring to a boil, stirring constantly. Then cook without stirring until a small amount dropped in very cold water forms a soft ball (232°). Add butter and remove from heat. Cool to lukewarm (110°). Beat until thick and creamy and of a nice spreading consistency. Keep over hot water while spreading.

Rocky Road Fudge Bars

Rich and irresistible. They are best made at least 24 hours before serving.

Bottom Layer:

Yield: 2 dozen

- ½ cup margarine
- 1 ounce unsweetened chocolate
- 1 cup flour
- 1 cup sugar
- 1 teaspoon baking powder
- 1 teaspoon vanilla
- 2 eggs, beaten
- ¾ cup chopped nuts

Melt margarine and chocolate in microwave (or in a small saucepan over low heat, stirring constantly). Add remaining ingredients and mix well. Spread in a greased and floured 9x13-inch baking pan.

Filling:

- 6 ounces softened cream cheese
- ¼ cup softened margarine
- ½ cup sugar
- 2 tablespoons all-purpose flour
- ½ teaspoon vanilla
- 1 egg, beaten
- ¼ cup chopped nuts
- 6 ounces semi-sweet chocolate chips
- 2 cups miniature marshmallows

Combine cream cheese, margarine and sugar. Add flour, vanilla and egg and beat until smooth and light. Stir in nuts. Spread over batter in pan and sprinkle with chocolate chips. Bake at 350° for 25-35 minutes or until toothpick inserted in center comes out clean. Immediately sprinkle marshmallows on top and return to oven for 2 minutes.

Frosting:

- 2 ounces cream cheese
- ¼ cup margarine
- ¼ cup milk
- 1 ounce unsweetened chocolate
- 1 teaspoon vanilla
- 3 cups sifted confectioners sugar

In a medium saucepan, combine cream cheese, margarine, milk, and chocolate. Cook and stir over low heat until blended. Remove from heat and stir in vanilla and confectioners sugar. Beat until smooth. Pour frosting over marshmallows and swirl with a knife. Refrigerate until firm. Cut into bars to serve.

Juan Seguin was at times considered a traitor by Texas, and at other times by Mexico. The San Antonio-born soldier commanded the only detachment of Texas-born Mexicans in the Texas Army at the Battle of San Jacinto in 1836. After serving in the Texas Senate and as mayor of San Antonio, he went to Mexico, joined the Mexican Army and returned to San Antonio as part of the invading army that briefly recaptured San Antonio 6 years after Texas had won its independence from Mexico at San Jacinto. He received permission from Sam Houston to return to Texas in 1848. The town of Seguin is named for him.

Layered Rum Brownies

Each layer of these delicious brownies must be completely cool before the next layer is added. They are better the second day.

Yield: 24 servings

First Layer:

1 **12.9-ounce package brownie mix (bake as directed on box)**
1 **cup chopped nuts**
2 **tablespoons rum**

Follow directions on box to make brownies, adding nuts. Spread rum over top of baked brownies while still hot. Refrigerate.

Second Layer:

4 **tablespoons melted butter**
1¾ **cups confectioners sugar**
2 **tablespoons rum**

Mix ingredients together until of spreading consistency. Spread over brownies and refrigerate.

Third Layer:

1 **6-ounce package chocolate chips**
1 **tablespoon butter**
   Milk

Melt chocolate chips and butter in top of a double boiler or in the microwave. Stir until smooth. Add milk by teaspoons until of spreading consistency. Spread over second layer and refrigerate.

Chocolate-Mint Brownies

The mint adds a new touch to an old favorite.

Yield: 2 dozen

½ cup soft butter or margarine
1 cup sugar
4 eggs, beaten
1 teaspoon vanilla
½ teaspoon salt
1 cup all-purpose flour
1½ cups chocolate syrup
½ cup chopped pecans

Cream butter or margarine and sugar until smooth. Stir in eggs and vanilla. Sift salt and flour together and mix into egg mixture. Add chocolate syrup and pecans; mix thoroughly. Pour batter into an oiled 9x13-inch cake pan and bake at 350° for 25 minutes.

Filling:

2 cups powdered sugar
4 tablespoons melted butter or margarine
1½ teaspoons mint extract
3-4 drops green food coloring
1-2 tablespoons milk

Mix sugar, melted butter or margarine, mint extract and food coloring together until smooth. Add milk slowly, stirring until filling becomes creamy. Spread evenly over brownies. Chill.

Frosting:

2 tablespoons butter
5 ounces semi-sweet baking chocolate

Melt butter and baking chocolate in microwave or in a small pan over boiling water. Stir until smooth and glossy. Spread evenly over mint filling. Chill until set.

Variation: Substitute 2 teaspoons creme de menthe for the mint extract and you will have Grasshopper Brownies.

Sweets and Treats

One hundred years ago the Texas Panhandle was considered the edge of the Great American Desert. Because there were no trees for lumber, early settlers often lived in dugouts and sod houses and burned cow chips for cooking and warmth. Some early settlers to the area managed to bring their family portraits and pianos as symbols of their previous lifestyles. Only with the coming of the railroad and windmill did life on the High Plains become any easier. Texas Tech University's Ranching Heritage Center, a 15-acre outdoor history museum, recreates the way it was on the Plains for those brave souls.

Peanutty Cookies

Yield: 3 dozen

1 cup sugar
¼ cup creamy peanut butter
¼ cup peanut oil
1 tablespoon butter or margarine
1 teaspoon vanilla
2 eggs, slightly beaten
1⅓ cups flour
1¼ teaspoons baking powder
¾ cup finely chopped peanuts

Cream sugar, peanut butter, oil and butter or margarine. Stir in vanilla and eggs. Combine flour and baking powder and blend into creamed mixture. Add ¼ cup chopped peanuts, reserving remaining ½ cup.

Chill dough for several hours or overnight. Form into walnut-size balls and roll in reserved chopped peanuts. Place 2 inches apart on a greased cookie sheet. Bake at 350° for 10-12 minutes or until golden brown. Remove from cookie sheet immediately and cool on a wire rack.

Sweets and Treats

The first recorded rattlesnake derby was held in the West Texas town of McCamey in April 1936. Thousands came to see Slicker, Esmeralda. Drain Pipe, Wonder Boy, Airflow and May Westian Rosie race for a $200 purse. Handlers placed their snakes in the starting box, the opening pistol roared and the box fell apart. Contestants writhed and squirmed in a big ball for a moment before separating and heading toward the finish line. Hundreds of cameras clicked as Slicker slithered across the line first.

More's Better Cookies

Yield: 5 dozen

1 cup shortening
¾ cup light brown sugar
¾ cup sugar
2 eggs
1½ cups all-purpose flour
1¼ teaspoons soda
1 teaspoon salt
1 cup chopped nuts (your preference)
¼ cup peanut butter chips
¼ cup butterscotch chips
1 6-ounce package chocolate chips
2 cups oatmeal (old-fashioned)
1 teaspoon vanilla
1 teaspoon hot water
1 cup coconut (optional)

Cream shortening and sugars together. Add eggs, one at a time. Sift flour, soda and salt together into egg mixture. Add nuts, chips, oatmeal, vanilla and hot water and stir. Add coconut if desired.

Roll cookie dough into 1-inch balls and place on an ungreased cookie sheet. Bake at 350° for 8-10 minutes.

Buffalo herds once migrated south in the winter through a gap in a small range of mountains in Taylor County. Knowing when the herds would be passing through, buffalo hunters would camp nearby, ready to kill the animals and then skin them on the spot. Eastern markets clamored for the pelts to make into lap robes—and for the smoked bison tongues, which they considered a delicacy. Slaughter of the largest of North America's native mammals reached its peak about 1875, with as many as 100,000 hides sold at Fort Worth in one day. By 1885 the buffalo from which the west Texas town of Buffalo Gap acquired its name had become an endangered species.

Buffalo Chips

They're great big delicious cookies.

Yield: 4-5 dozen

1 pound butter or margarine
2 cups packed brown sugar
2 cups white sugar
4 eggs
4 cups flour
2 teaspoons baking powder
2 teaspoons baking soda
2 cups crushed corn flakes
1 12-ounce package chocolate chips
2 cups chopped pecans or walnuts
2 cups quick oatmeal, uncooked

Melt butter and cool to lukewarm. Add sugars and mix well. Add remaining ingredients in order given, stirring after each addition.

Use an ice cream scoop to measure amount of cookie dough for each cookie. Place 6 scoops only on each ungreased cookie sheet. Bake at 350° for 13-15 minutes.

Sweets and Treats

That Houston exists at all today, much less as a great metropolis, is due to the "overcomer" persistence of its founders, the flamboyant promoters A.C. and J.K. Allen. After trying unsuccessfully to buy the nearby town of Harrisburg, A.C. Allen paddled his canoe up Buffalo Bayou, sounding its depth frequently until he arrived at what seemed to be the farthest navigable point upstream for commercial boats. He sat on the grassy bank and sketched out a map of his dream city on a scrap of paper, using his hat for a pad — mud, mosquitos, alligators, Indians, yellow fever and Harrisburg be damned!

Nancy Jo's No-Bake Cookies

A friend who says she never has time to cook sent the recipe for these simple-to-make cookies that are delicious and take only minutes to prepare.

Yield: 4 dozen

2 cups sugar
6 tablespoons cocoa
½ cup milk
1 tablespoon butter or margarine
½ cup peanut butter
3 cups 1-minute oatmeal

Mix sugar and cocoa in a large saucepan. Add milk gradually and stir until cocoa is moistened. Bring to a boil over medium heat. Remove and add butter or margarine, peanut butter and oatmeal. Mix thoroughly. Drop by teaspoon on *wax paper* and let cool. These keep well when stored in an airtight container in the refrigerator.

Hallettsville, county seat of Lavaca County in south-central Texas, had a taste of national fame long before its beautiful old courthouse and square were seen in scenes of the movie "The Best Little Whorehouse in Texas." Robert Ripley included the little town in his *Believe It Or Not* tales, citing the prevalence of the number 13 in its makeup — 13 letters in the name Hallettsville, which "with 1,300 people in 1913, had 13 newspapers, 13 saloons, and 13 churches." The courthouse square has always been the gathering point for community visiting, and old-timers recall Saturdays when groups of area residents would be speaking only German on one side of the courthouse, only Czech on a second, and only English on another.

Brown Sugar Kisses

An old family recipe that is a treasure. These little cookies are easy to make and delicious to eat.

Yield: 30 cookies

1 egg white
1 cup brown sugar, sifted by forcing through a coarse sieve with a wooden spoon
1 teaspoon vanilla
2 cups coarsely chopped pecans

Beat egg white until stiff but not dry. Add brown sugar and continue beating until thoroughly mixed. Add vanilla and pecans and stir. Drop by teaspoon on a greased cookie sheet and bake for 5-6 minutes in 400° oven. Allow to cool for 10 minutes before removing from cookie sheet.

Tip: *If brown sugar hardens, place it and an apple wedge in an airtight container for 24 hours.*

SWEETS AND TREATS

During the mid-1800's Texas Rangers regularly rode the winding, 100-mile trail between San Antonio and Kerrville to protect surrounding settlements from Indian attack. The town of Bandera was located midway on the trail; and because Indians often ambushed travelers at nearby Bandera Pass, the town became a Ranger outpost. In 1841 Capt. Jack Hays and 40 Rangers defeated several hundred Comanches at Bandera Pass. In time the route came to be called the Texas Ranger Trail.

Karen's Oatmeal Cookies

These won't last long if you have cookie eaters around.

Yield: 5-6 dozen

1 cup shortening
1 cup sugar
1 cup brown sugar
2 eggs
1 teaspoon vanilla
1 teaspoon butter flavoring
1½ cups all-purpose flour
1 teaspoon salt
1 teaspoon soda
3 teaspoons cinnamon
3 cups oatmeal
1 cup chopped pecans
  or peanuts
¼ cup wheat germ
½ cup sunflower seed kernels
  (optional)

Cream shortening and sugars in a large bowl. Add eggs, vanilla and flavoring. Sift flour, salt, soda and cinnamon into creamed mixture and stir until smooth. Mix oatmeal into batter, one cup at a time. Add nuts, wheat germ and sunflower seed kernels (optional) and stir until dough is blended.

Drop rounded teaspoons of batter 1 inch apart on greased cookie sheets and bake at 350° for 10-12 minutes. Wait 5 minutes before removing from cookie sheet.

Bomma's Date Nut Cookies

Yield: 5 dozen

¾ cup sugar
½ cup flour
½ teaspoon baking powder
¼ teaspoon salt
1 pound chopped dates
2 cups chopped pecans
¼ teaspoon vanilla
3 egg whites, stiffly beaten

Combine dry ingredients and mix with dates, pecans and vanilla in a large bowl. Mix in egg whites. Drop by teaspoonful onto a greased cookie sheet. Bake at 325° for 15 minutes.

Walk-To-School Cookies

These refrigerator cookies have a wonderful texture. The Midland contributor did not give the reason for their name, but it sounds as if they seldom made it to school in the lunch box.

Yield: About 6 dozen

2 cups butter or margarine
1 cup sugar
1 teaspoon vanilla
4 cups all-purpose flour
½ cup chopped pecans
Confectioners sugar

Cream butter or margarine and sugar together. Add vanilla and mix. Stir in flour and pecans, mixing with hands when dough becomes stiff. Press and mold into 3 long rolls about 2½ inches in diameter. Wrap in waxed paper and chill for several hours. Slice about ½-inch thick and place on an ungreased cookie sheet. Bake at 350° for 10-12 minutes. Sprinkle with confectioners sugar while slightly warm. Keep the unbaked portion in the refrigerator for freshly baked cookies several days later.

Y'all's Texas Cheese Torte

This Wisialowski family recipe is a melt-in-your-mouth dessert that can be served alone or smothered with fresh berries.

Yield: 8-10 servings

Graham Cracker Crust:

- ¾ **cup graham cracker crumbs, finely crushed**
- ¼ **cup melted butter or margarine**
- 2 **teaspoons sugar**

Filling:

- 2 **pounds large-curd cottage cheese**
- 1½ **cups sugar**
- 3 **tablespoons all-purpose flour**
- 6 **eggs**
- ½ **pint sour cream**
- ¼ **teaspoon salt**
- 1 **teaspoon vanilla**
- ¼ **cup milk**

Place graham cracker crumbs in a medium bowl. Add sugar and melted butter or margarine to crumbs and mix. Reserve ¼ cup crumb mixture for topping torte. Butter sides of a 9-inch springform pan and press remaining crumb mixture on sides and bottom of pan.

Combine all ingredients in a large blender or food processor bowl and beat until smooth. (You may need to divide filling for blending since mixture could be too much for one blender bowl.) Pour filling over graham cracker crust and sprinkle reserved graham cracker mixture over top of filling. Bake for 1 hour at 350° or until torte tests done. Serve chilled, y'all.

The Gulf Intracoastal Waterway is the busiest "river" in Texas, hugging the Texas coastline for 423 miles from Port Isabel to Sabine Pass, and then continuing to Florida. The first stretch opened in 1913 between Galveston and Corpus Christi. Chugging tugboats haul barges filled with petroleum products, chemicals, cement, agricultural products and even space vehicles and missiles along the route. The Waterway is 12 to 14 feet deep and from 100 to 125 feet wide.

Italian Cheesecake

This delicate, lemony cheesecake will bring rave reviews.

Yield: 12 servings

Graham cracker crumbs
2 15-ounce cartons Ricotta cheese
1 cup sugar
5 egg yolks
⅓ cup sifted all-purpose flour
Grated rind of 1 large lemon
⅔ teaspoon vanilla
5 egg whites
⅓ cup sugar
⅓ cup whipping cream (optional)

Butter a 9-inch springform pan and sprinkle with graham cracker crumbs. Use an electric mixer, a food processor or a blender to beat Ricotta cheese until smooth. Gradually add sugar and egg yolks, beating after each addition. Beat in flour, grated lemon rind and vanilla.

Beat egg white in a medium bowl until frothy; add sugar and continue beating until stiff but not dry. Beat whipping cream until stiff and fold it and egg white into Ricotta mixture and turn into the prepared springform pan.

Bake in preheated 450° oven for first 10 minutes; lower temperature to 350° and bake for 1 hour longer. Turn off heat and allow to cool in oven with door closed. Sprinkle top with confectioners sugar.

Delicious Applesauce Spice Bars

Yield: 24 bars

2 cups flour, sifted
2 teaspoons soda
¾ teaspoon cinnamon
¼ teaspoon cloves
¼ teaspoon nutmeg
½ teaspoon salt
½ cup soft butter
1 cup sugar
1 egg
1 teaspoon vanilla
1½ cups applesauce
1 cup pecans
1 cup raisins

Sift first six ingredients together. Mix butter and sugar together and add flour mixture and rest of the ingredients. Pour into 9x13-inch pan and bake at 350° for 25 minutes. Cool and frost with Caramel Frosting.

Caramel Frosting:

½ cup butter
1 cup brown sugar
¼ cup milk
2 cups powdered sugar
1 teaspoon vanilla
Dash of salt

Cook butter and sugar for 2 minutes. Add milk and just bring to a boil. Add powdered sugar, vanilla and salt and beat until of spreading consistency. Spread over top of Applesauce Bars.

SWEETS AND TREATS

The United States Air Force had its humble beginnings at San Antonio's Fort Sam Houston in 1910 when Lt. Benjamin Foulois arrived with several crates filled with bamboo poles and a gasoline engine. Congress had given him a once-wrecked Wright Brothers plane and $150 to fix it up. He began to teach himself to fly with the help of a correspondence course with Orville and Wilbur Wright. On March 2 the plane, with Foulois at the controls, was hurled from a catapult for a brief but successful flight. He later wrote, "The lack of a rear stabilizer caused the old plane to buck like a Texas cow pony." He went on to become Chief of the Army Air Corps.

Buttermilk-Pecan Pie

Yield: 7 servings

½ cup butter or margarine
2 cups sugar
3 eggs
2 teaspoons vanilla
3 tablespoons all-purpose flour
¼ teaspoon salt
1 cup buttermilk
½ cup chopped pecans
1 9-inch unbaked pie shell

Cream butter or margarine and sugar together, adding sugar gradually. Add eggs one at a time. Blend in vanilla, flour and salt. Add buttermilk and mix gently. Sprinkle pecans in pie crust and pour custard mixture over pecans. (Pecans will come to the top as the pie bakes.) Bake in a preheated 300° oven for 1½ hours. Test by inserting a knife in center of pie.

SWEETS AND TREATS

The Big Bend ghost town of Terlingua, near the Mexican border, has only a few dozen full-time residents. In the 1890's it was a boom town of 2,000 people drawn there by the mining of cinnabar, used in the manufacture of quicksilver. Today this dusty little town attracts thousands of "chili heads" for the November annual World Championship Chili Cook-Off, where showmanship is the number-one ingredient. For those with fainter hearts and palates, Terlingua also hosts a Cookie Chill-Off each February during the Big Bend bluebonnet and desert flower season.

Mint Mist Pie

This refreshing desert dessert was the winner of the 1987 Terlingua Cookie Chill-Off. The mint is a perfect antidote for any chili left from the Chili Cook-off.

Yield: 12 servings

Crust:

1 13-ounce package pecan shortbread cookies (reserve ½ cup)

6 tablespoons melted butter or margarine

Combine cookie crumbs and butter or margarine, mixing well. Press in bottom of a 9-inch springform pan.

Filling:

8 ounces cream cheese

1 14-ounce can sweetened *condensed* milk

1 teaspoon mint extract
Few drops green food coloring

8 ounces non-dairy whipped topping

⅔ cup miniature chocolate chips

Beat cream cheese until light and fluffy. Gradually add condensed milk, mint extract and food coloring and beat until smooth. Fold in whipped topping with a spatula. Fold in chocolate chips. Spoon filling into pie crust. Freeze overnight or for at least 8 hours. Remove from freezer 5 minutes before serving. Sprinkle reserved cookie crumbs over top and garnish with fresh mint.

The Llano Estacado, or Staked Plains, is almost perfectly flat and treeless from edge to edge. It covers most of the Texas Panhandle and crosses into New Mexico. Some say the Staked Plains were so named because horses had to be "staked" since there were no trees to tie them to; or because the Cap Rock appears palisaded in many places; or even because "Estacado" is a corruption of Destacado, meaning elevated. The Plains are so flat that Francisco Coronado's followers on their quest for gold in 1541 noted they could see blue sky through the legs of a distant buffalo herd.

Chocolate Chess Pie

A wonderful, chocolaty pie that belongs on that list of ALL-TIME FAVORITES.

Yield: 7 servings

½ cup butter
½ cup water
¼ cup cocoa
4 egg yolks
1 whole egg, slightly beaten
1½ cups sugar
1 teaspoon vanilla
1 9-inch unbaked pie crust

Combine butter and water in a small saucepan and bring to a boil. Add cocoa and mix. Set aside to cool. Beat egg yolks and egg with sugar. Add cooled cocoa mixture and vanilla and blend. Pour into pie crust and bake at 350° on lowest oven rack for 45-55 minutes or until set but still soft. If pie is browning too fast, lower oven temperature to 300°. Chill several hours before serving.

Sweets and Treats

The Great Depression in the early 30's spawned one of the most notorious legends in Texas history, that of Bonnie and Clyde. The infamous Clyde Barrow and his gun-toting moll left a wake of terror throughout the state with their robberies, gunfights and murders. They were killed in 1934 in an ambush in Louisiana participated in by a deputy who had admired the pretty blond waitress in her pre-gangster days as she served his daily lunch at a cafe near the Dallas County Courthouse. Bonnie had been with the Barrow gang two years when she died at 23.

Carrot Pie

A corner gift shop in Lancaster (M. Ruth Company) occupies the building that was originally the Henry Bank, robbed by Bonnie and Clyde in 1933. The original bank vault is still there, filled with gifts, not money.

Yield: 7 servings

1½ cups cooked carrots
2 eggs, slightly beaten
¾ cup sugar
1½ teaspoons cinnamon
2 teaspoons nutmeg
¼ teaspoon salt
1 12-ounce can evaporated milk
1 tablespoon milk
1 9-inch unbaked pie shell

Mash and beat cooked carrots until smooth. Combine with eggs, sugar and seasonings. Add milks and mix. Pour into pie shell. Bake at 400° for 10 minutes. Lower heat to 350° and bake until a knife inserted in center comes out clean (30-40 minutes).

Sweets and Treats

One of the San Antonio River's most charming features is its meandering path through downtown San Antonio, where it travels 15 miles to cross 6 miles of city blocks. The stream's most colorful name dates to the first years of Spanish settlement, when local Indians (who by then had learned much more than the Christian virtues expounded by their padres) called the river by a native name which roughly translates to "drunken old man going home at night."

Margarita Pie

Yield: 7 servings

Crust:
½ cup finely crushed pretzel crumbs
½ cup finely crushed graham cracker crumbs
1 tablespoon sugar
⅓ cup melted butter or margarine

Combine pretzel crumbs, graham cracker crumbs and sugar in a medium bowl. Add melted butter or margarine and mix well. Reserve 2 tablespoons of mixture for topping on pie. Press remaining crumbs into bottom of a buttered 9-inch pie pan.

Filling:
4 egg yolks
2 tablespoons sugar
1 envelope unflavored gelatin
1 6-ounce can frozen limeade concentrate, thawed
2-3 drops green food coloring
1 3-ounce package softened cream cheese
¼ cup tequila
2 tablespoons triple sec
4 egg whites
¼ cup sugar
1 lime, thinly sliced

Combine egg yolks and sugar in top of a double boiler and beat until thick. Mix gelatin with limeade and add to double boiler. Stir constantly over boiling water until mixture begins to thicken. Remove from heat and add coloring to give a pale green color. Beat cream cheese until light, add ½ cup of egg yolk mixture and beat. Blend in remaining egg yolk mixture, tequila and triple sec.

Beat egg whites until frothy; gradually add sugar. Fold creamed mixture into egg whites and pile into crust. Sprinkle with reserved crumbs and garnish with thin slices of lime.

Sweets and Treats

Successful farming in early Texas required special techniques not necessarily related to the actual growing process. As one Texian later related: "I hired a young man to live with me. We would take our guns with us to the field to plow, and we would leave one gun at one end of the rows and one at the other; then we ploughed so that he would be at one end and I at the other, so that the Indians could not cut us off from both our guns."

Pineapple Pie — Texas Style

This has been a four-generation favorite of one Williamson County family. Joanne Matysek Land says her father, who was Williamson County Sheriff for 20 years, thought no family gathering was complete without at least one Pineapple Pie.

Yield: 7 servings

1 20-ounce can crushed pineapple
½ teaspoon salt
¾ cup sugar
2 tablespoons cornstarch
2 egg yolks
1 tablespoon lemon juice
2 tablespoons butter
1 unbaked double pie shell
Cinnamon and sugar

Mix pineapple, salt, sugar and cornstarch in a medium saucepan. Cook and stir over medium heat until mixture thickens and becomes clear. Beat egg yolks, add to pineapple mixture and cook for 1 minute. Remove from heat and add lemon juice. Pour into an unbaked pie shell and dot with butter. Make a lattice on top of pineapple filling with the other pie crust. Sprinkle liberally with cinnamon and sugar. Bake at 350° for 30-35 minutes.

Back when cotton was undisputed king of the Texas economy, cottonpatch super-stitions abounded, including the following:

If a young man sits on a cotton bale with his legs crossed, he will be blessed with many children. Good luck comes to those couples who make love while picking cotton. Wherever a whirlwind drops a cotton boll, there you will find money. Always pick the first boll of cotton that opens in a field, carry it home, put it over the front door, pick out the seeds of the boll and plant them under the back doorstep. You will get good prices for your cotton if you do this, but woe unto you if you don't.

Clifton Cocoa Pie

This family recipe came with the quote that "it's absolutely wicked it's so good." It's rich and chocolaty and has a wonderful meringue.

Yield: 7 pieces

Cocoa Pie:

2 cups milk
3 egg yolks (reserve whites for meringue)
1½ cups sugar
⅓-½ cup cocoa
¼ cup cornstarch or flour
¾ teaspoon salt
2 teaspoons vanilla
1 baked 9-inch pie crust

Heat 1½ cups milk in a medium saucepan. Mix remaining ½ cup milk with egg yolks; add sugar, cocoa, flour and salt. Combine with hot milk and cook over low heat, stirring constantly, until thickened. Remove from heat, add vanilla and pour into baked pie crust. Top with meringue.

Meringue:

3 egg whites
½ teaspoon baking powder
6 tablespoons sugar

Beat egg whites and baking powder until frothy. Add sugar gradually and continue beating until stiff and glossy. Swirl meringue on pie filling and bake at 350° for 12-15 minutes.

SWEETS AND TREATS

Nacogdoches was the base for the short-lived "Republic of Fredonia" in 1827. Adventurer Hayden Edwards, furious about misunderstandings over his colonization contract with the Mexican government, declared his East Texas territory independent of Mexico and named it Fredonia. Stephen F. Austin's colonists, plus most of the rest of Nacogdoches, refused to support Edwards and his small band. Mexican troops quickly crushed the Fredonian Rebellion, and Edwards and his brother fled to the United States.

Fredonia Pie

The Fredonia Hotel is a landmark in Nacogdoches, one of the oldest towns in Texas. The hotel is being renovated and refurbished and will open early in 1988 as The Fredonia Hotel and Convention Center.

Yield: 7 servings

First you put 1½ cups sugar and 1 stick butter in a bowl

Run your hand mixer a minute or so until creamy

Eggs are next, break 3 into mixture and beat well

Don't forget to add 3 rounded tablespoons flour

One teaspoon vanilla extract goes in

Next add 1 cup buttermilk

I won't tell anyone it's buttermilk if you won't

All that's left is to pour into an unbaked 9-inch pie shell

Please sprinkle nutmeg on top before baking

I set the oven at 350° and bake for 1 hour

Everyone raves over this pie!

Sherman is now as sedate a town as they come, but it wasn't back in 1857 when rowdies tore down the first county courthouse to settle a bet as to whether an old grey duck had her nest under the log building. We don't know whether she did or not; but we do know that when the sheriff came along the next day to post a legal notice on the courthouse door, he dug the door from the debris, propped it up, and posted his notice accordingly.

Chocolate-Mint Mousse

Yield: 6 servings

1 tablespoon unflavored gelatin
½ cup water
2 1-ounce squares unsweetened baking chocolate
8 chocolate-covered mint wafers
⅔ cup sugar
1 cup scalded milk
1¾ cups whipping cream
1 teaspoon vanilla
⅓ cup chopped slivered almonds or chopped pecans (optional)

Soak gelatin in ¼ cup of the water in a medium bowl. Heat the other ¼ cup and chocolate in the top of a double boiler until chocolate is melted. Add mint wafers and stir until melted. Blend in sugar and milk. Pour over gelatin and mix well. Refrigerate until slightly thickened.

Whip cream until thick and glossy. Reserve 1 cup for topping. Add vanilla to chocolate mixture and fold into whipped cream. Pour into a mold or individual serving dishes. Top with reserved whipped cream and sprinkle with nuts (if desired).

Note: If you are counting calories or watching cholesterol, non-dairy whipped topping works fine in place of whipped cream.

Trust and hospitality usually walk hand in hand. Just 50 years ago customers at God's Mercy Store in Waller paid the dealer's cost on all goods purchased, plus whatever extra they deemed proper as a freewill offering. Pearsall's Mercantile Hotel operated without a desk clerk. Guests selected their own rooms, put their payment in an envelope and dropped it in a box as they left. Both establishments operated at a profit for many years.

Chocolate-Mocha Dessert Crepes

Yield: Ten 6-inch crepes

1 tablespoon cocoa
½ cup all-purpose flour
2 teaspoons sugar
⅛ teaspoon salt
¾ cup milk
½ teaspoon vanilla
1 egg
2 teaspoons melted butter or margarine
Vegetable oil

Combine cocoa, flour, sugar and salt. Mix in milk and vanilla. Add egg and beat until smooth. Mix in butter or margarine and refrigerate for a minimum of 1 hour.

Brush a thin coating of oil in bottom of a crepe pan or an 8-inch skillet and heat. Pour 2 tablespoons batter in bottom of pan and tilt pan so batter spreads over entire bottom of pan. Cook crepe quickly on both sides. Remove and place on a plate to cool.

To serve, fill with coffee ice cream, roll and top with Homemade Chocolate Sauce.

Homemade Chocolate Sauce:

2 cups sugar
1 12-ounce can evaporated milk
4 squares unsweetened chocolate, melted
½ cup butter or margarine
1 teaspoon vanilla
½ teaspoon salt

Boil sugar and evaporated milk in a heavy saucepan for 2 minutes. Add melted chocolate and beat until smooth. Add butter or margarine, vanilla and salt and mix well.

Shortly after the battle at the Alamo in March 1836, Col. James W. Fannin's garrison was massacred while withdrawing from the old Spanish Fort Presidio La Bahia at Goliad. After having declined to go to the Alamo's aid, Fannin was also tardy in obeying Sam Houston's order to retreat to Victoria. When Fannin's 400-man force did leave La Bahia, it was attacked by General Urrea's Mexican army. Fannin surrendered, believing he and his men would be treated humanely. Instead, a week later the Mexican army was ordered to fire on their prisoners and all except some 30 who managed to escape were killed. This so inflamed what remained of the Texian army that the battle cry at San Jacinto was "Remember the Alamo, Remember Goliad."

Goliad Bread Pudding

The aroma of this old-fashioned bread pudding will bring everyone within sniffing distance running to see what's in the oven.

Yield: 8 servings

12 slices white bread
1 stick butter or margarine
1 teaspoon cinnamon
½-1 cup raisins
4 cups milk
1 cup white sugar
3 eggs
1 teaspoon vanilla

Spread bread slices generously with butter or margarine and cut each slice into quarters. Place half of bread in bottom of a 9x13-inch baking dish. Sprinkle with half of the cinnamon and raisins. Make a second layer using remaining bread, cinnamon and raisins.

Heat milk. Add sugar, eggs and vanilla and stir until sugar is dissolved. Pour milk mixture over bread. Set baking dish in shallow pan of hot water and bake at 350° for 45 minutes. Serve with Bread Pudding Sauce.

Bread Pudding Sauce:

½ cup butter or margarine
⅔ cup light cream or
   evaporated milk
⅓ cup white sugar

Combine ingredients in medium saucepan. Cook and stir over medium heat until creamy. Ladle over top of each serving of pudding.

Glenda's Good Southern Cobbler

Peaches or frozen blackberries may be used in this simple-to-make dessert. Top with vanilla ice cream and you have a Texas favorite.

Yield: 6 servings

1 cup all-purpose flour
1 cup sugar
1 cup milk
1 teaspoon baking powder
Dash of salt
2 tablespoons melted butter or margarine
2 cups sliced fresh peaches (or 2 cups fresh or frozen blackberries, sweetened to taste)

Mix all ingredients except fruit in a 2-quart greased baking dish. Spoon peaches and juice over top of batter; do not stir. Bake for 35-45 minutes at 350° or until golden brown.

Lazy Scout Cobbler

A great recipe to make in a dutch oven over an open camp fire.

Yield: 6-8 servings

1 stick margarine
1 cup sugar
1 cup self-rising flour
1 cup milk
1 16-ounce can fruit pie filling (cherry, apple, blueberry, etc.)

Melt butter in the pan you are going to cook cobbler in. Mix sugar and flour in a medium bowl, add milk gradually and stir until blended. Pour fruit in pan with melted butter. Pour batter over fruit and butter. Do not stir. Bake in a 400° oven until brown on top (25-30 minutes).

Sweets and Treats

The Lyndon Baines Johnson National Historic Park is situated in the heart of the Texas Hill Country. The Pedernales River winds past 100-year-old live oak and pecan trees that shade the boyhood home of President Johnson. Texas longhorns, white-tailed deer and buffalo, a replica of the frontier farm, the LBJ ranch that served as the Texas White House, and the President's grave are all part of the Park. It is a fascinating blend of a simpler time in early Texas and the complexity of life in the most demanding job in the United States.

Lady Bird's Peach Ice Cream

Mrs. Lyndon B. Johnson comments about this recipe: "With our Stonewall peaches this makes our very favorite company dessert — a summer treat without equal."

Yield: 1 gallon

1 cup sugar
3 eggs, slightly beaten
1 pint milk
1 quart cream
2 quarts ripe, juicy peaches, mashed and well sweetened (amount of sugar needed will vary with sweetness of peaches)

Mix sugar and eggs in a large saucepan. Add milk, stir and bring to a simmer over medium heat. Cook until slightly thickened. Add cream and cool. Add sweetened mashed peaches. Place in an ice cream freezer can and chill for 1 hour. Freeze following directions for your ice cream freezer. Allow ice cream to ripen for 2-3 hours before serving.

Sweets and Treats

These days charcoal is seldom seen outside the barbeque grill. But not so in days past when it was used to insulate ice boxes, in toothpaste, as chewing gum flavoring, and to filter and purify water. Tailors and tinsmiths used it to heat their irons, and nurserymen when planting flowers. An old-time Bandera saloonkeeper offered this cure: "I had stomach trouble bad. I cured it by eating powdered cedar charcoal mixed with honey. I have passed this information on to many of my friends, and it has helped all of them—that has tried it."

Watermelon Sorbet

A light, cool dessert for a hot summer night.

Yield: 6-8 servings

4 **cups watermelon chunks**
2 **tablespoons orange juice**
¼ **cup sugar**
2 **egg whites, stiffly beaten**
    Additional sugar if needed

Place watermelon chunks in a food processor or blender bowl. Purée until smooth. Remove seeds with a slotted spoon. You should have about 3 cups watermelon purée.

Add orange juice and sugar. Mix thoroughly and pour into a large flat bowl. Freeze until solid around edges but still slushy in the center. Stir until smooth. Taste, adding more sugar to egg whites if needed. Beat egg whites until stiff. Fold into sorbet. Freeze for 1-1½ hours without stirring. Serve in individual sherbet dishes or in small dessert bowls.

Wagon Wheel of Fruit

The bottom crust is similar to a shortbread, the second layer is a smooth creamy filling and the top layer consists of various fruits arranged like spokes of a wheel. It's an attractive and unusual dessert.

Yield: 12 servings

Crust:

½ cup confectioners sugar
½ cup sugar
½ cup corn oil
½ cup margarine
1 egg
2¼ cups all-purpose flour
½ teaspoon soda
½ teaspoon cream of tartar
½ teaspoon vanilla
Dash of salt

Combine ingredients, mixing thoroughly, and press evenly on a 14-inch pizza pan. Bake at 350° for 20 minutes or until golden brown.

Filling:

1 8-ounce package
cream cheese
½ cup sugar
1 teaspoon vanilla
1 cup non-dairy whipped topping (such as Cool Whip)

Combine cream cheese, sugar and vanilla, mixing well. Fold in non-dairy whipped topping. Spread evenly on baked crust.

Fruit Topping:

Fresh fruits (strawberries, peaches, pineapple, kiwi fruit, bananas, etc.)

Arrange fruit in narrow spokes from center to edge of filling. Vary fruits so that colors and textures make an attractive plate.

Glaze:

½ cup fruit juice
2 tablespoons lemon juice
1 tablespoon cornstarch
¼ cup water
⅓ cup sugar

Mix glaze ingredients in a medium saucepan and cook, stirring frequently, over medium heat until thickened and clear. Spoon over top of fruit. Chill until serving time.

Light Fruit Compote

This fresh-tasting fruit compote is low in sugar and calories and so good you'll be happy to forego both.

Yield: 8 servings

1 16-ounce can pear halves in own juice (or in light syrup), chopped

1 20-ounce can pineapple chunks in own juice

1 16-ounce can fruit cocktail in light syrup

1 10-ounce package frozen sliced, unsweetened strawberries, thawed

½ cup drained maraschino cherries

2 apples, cored and diced

2 bananas, sliced

1 1.1-ounce package vanilla sugar-free instant pudding

Drain canned fruits, reserving juices, and place in a large bowl. Add strawberries, cherries, apples and bananas. Mix pudding with reserved juices, stirring until thoroughly dissolved. Combine pudding and fruit juice mixture with fruit and refrigerate for several hours before serving.

Fresh Fruit Ambrosia

Yield: 6 servings

2 large oranges

1 fresh ripe pineapple

2 bananas

¼ cup sugar

2 tablespoons rum
Dash salt

¾ cup shredded coconut

Peel oranges with a sharp knife; cut crosswise into thin slices about ¼-inch thick. Pare pineapple, core and cut into bite-size chunks. Slice bananas and combine with oranges, pineapple, sugar, rum and salt in a large bowl. Chill for 1 hour. Top with coconut and mint leaves just before serving.

Sweets and Treats

Corpus Christi is Texas' "Sparkling City by the Sea," and the surrounding area, called the Texas Riviera, is the favorite vacation spot for many Texans. The seafood, the beaches, the shrimp boats, the Padre Island National Park across the bridge, nearby Aransas Wild Life Refuge—all combine to offer opportunities to do a lot or to do nothing. The area was first mapped in 1519 by Alonzo de Pineda, who possibly died there of wounds received in a fight with the Karankawa Indians.

Uncle Max's Microwave Peanut Brittle

Yield: 1 pound

1 cup raw peanuts
1 cup granulated sugar
½ cup white corn syrup
⅛ teaspoon salt
1 teaspoon butter or margarine
1 teaspoon vanilla
1 teaspoon baking soda

Combine peanuts, sugar, corn syrup and salt in a 2-quart glass bowl or measuring cup. Mix thoroughly with a wooden spoon. Place bowl with ingredients and wooden spoon in microwave oven and cook on High for 8 minutes, stirring well after 4 minutes. (Use hot pads when touching bowl and spoon as they will be very hot.) Add butter or margarine and vanilla, return to oven and cook on High for 2 minutes. Peanuts will be lightly browned and syrup will be *very* hot.

Add baking soda and gently stir until light and foamy. Let syrup rise. When it stops, pour mixture on a lightly greased large pizza pan or flexible cookie sheet. When cool, bend pan to remove brittle in large pieces. Wipe excess oil from undersides. Break into small pieces and store in an airtight container. If kept in a cool place, candy will keep for several weeks.

Chocolate Roasted Pecan Clusters

Yield: 3½ dozen

3 tablespoons butter
3 cups pecan pieces
1 pound sweet chocolate
1 14-ounce can sweetened
    condensed milk

Melt butter in a large broiler or jelly roll pan. Spread pecans evenly in pan. Bake at 300° for 30 minutes, stirring occasionally.

Melt chocolate in top of double boiler. Remove from heat and stir in milk. Add pecans and stir until well coated. Drop by teaspoonfuls onto waxed paper or a greased cookie sheet. Refrigerate for several hours.

Variation: Substitute ¾ pound almond bark for chocolate and eliminate condensed milk to make Roasted Pecan Bark Clusters.

Date Loaf Candy

Yield: 2 pounds

3 cups sugar
1½ cups milk
1 8-ounce package pitted
    dates
2 tablespoons butter
1 cup chopped pecans

Mix all ingredients except pecans in a medium saucepan. Cook until syrup forms a firm ball when tested in cold water (245-248° on a candy thermometer). Remove from heat and add pecans. Beat until thick and creamy. Turn out on a clean, damp dishtowel and form into a long loaf. Roll up and let stand until cool. Cut into ½-inch slices.

Signs and superstitions governed the actions of many Texas farmers well into the 20th Century. For example, cotton was planted "when the whippoorwill cries." The worm, or bottom rail, of a log fence was laid when the moon was waning so it wouldn't sink or rot. And the first frost would arrive 4 weeks after a farmer heard the first cricket chirp in the fall.

Buttermilk Fudge

If you've never tasted buttermilk fudge, give this a try. It has a wonderful flavor.

Yield: 64 servings

2 cups sugar
1 cup buttermilk
½ cup light corn syrup
1 teaspoon soda
4 tablespoons margarine
1 teaspoon vanilla
1 cup pecan halves

Mix sugar, buttermilk, corn syrup and soda together in a large saucepan. Cook over low heat, stirring frequently, until mixture spins a thread (246° on a candy thermometer). Remove from heat and add margarine. Beat until creamy and thick. Add vanilla and pecan halves. Stir until mixture holds its shape. Drop by teaspoon on greased platter or wax paper.

Tastes & Tales

HOUSE SPECIALTIES

Metropolitan Texas

House Specialties

Although the Mexican Constitution provided for public schools, many private schools (called "cornfield" schools) sprang up in Anglo Texas before the Revolution. Teachers moved from one farmstead to the next, taking as pay whatever they could get. Average tuition was about $2 a month. Because children had to help their parents in the fields, school days were as uncertain as the weather. One teacher told of having to hire a team of oxen to haul his "salary" — a cartload of corn — 100 miles to the nearest market.

Peach Chutney

There are many different types of chutney, but this one is especially good served with chicken or ham. A small jar would make a memorable gift for a special friend.

Yield: 8 pints

25 large peaches, peeled and diced
2 cups diced dried fruit mix (apples, pears, apricots, etc.)
½ cup diced dried prunes
1 cup currants
1 cup golden seedless raisins
1½ cups diced onion
3 cloves garlic, crushed
2 tablespoons salt
2½ cups cider vinegar
4 cups light brown sugar
2 teaspoons nutmeg
1 teaspoon dry mustard
¼ teaspoon ground cloves

Combine fruit, raisins, currants and onion in a large, heavy kettle. Mix garlic with salt and add to the kettle. Add remaining ingredients and simmer for 45-50 minutes. Spoon into sterilized containers, cool and seal.

Variation: If fresh peaches are not available, apples or pears may be substituted as the main ingredient.

House Specialties

The Steamboat Hotel in Fredericksburg was built in 1852 by Captain Charles Nimitz. It is now a museum honoring his grandson, Admiral Chester W. Nimitz, who was Commander in Chief of the Pacific Fleet during World War II. Nearby is the Japanese Garden of Peace, a gift to the people of the United States from the people of Japan. The garden is in serene contrast to the tanks, fighter planes and guns, all preserved from the Pacific conflict, that line the History Walk of the Pacific War, a part of the museum complex. A Memorial Wall commemorates Americans killed in the Pacific and honors Admiral Nimitz's request that the Center be dedicated to all who served with him in World War II.

Cincpac Special

Admiral Nimitz's recipe for Old Fashioned Mix was developed when he was Commander in Chief of the Pacific, where liquor was rationed and rum was frequently the only kind available. The recipe was shared with us by his daughter.

Yield: 1 gallon

1 clean 1-gallon jug
3 quarts bourbon
¼ of a fifth of gold label rum
Simple syrup (sugar and water)
2 whole vanilla beans (optional)

Pour bourbon and rum into jug. Make a simple syrup by heating 2 cups sugar and ½ cup water in a small saucepan until sugar is dissolved. Add simple syrup to jug cautiously until presence of sugar can begin to be detected. Fill remainder of jug with water. Admiral Nimitz adds, "Desirable but not necessary: drop two whole vanilla beans into the jug to stay for many refills of jug. They last for years. Pour generous portions over ice and serve it forth."

Nimitz Cactus Fruit Jelly

Admiral Nimitz's mother's recipe for this delicacy came from his daughter, Catherine Lay, who said she found it on a "much-folded, tattered sheet of paper that had been in my file at least 35 years." She concluded by saying she thought whoever tested the recipe should be given "Extra-Hazardous-Duty Pay." The first part of the instructions is printed as Mrs. Nimitz wrote them long ago. (Ingredients in parentheses are added for clarification.) For the cooking of the jelly, we suggest you use instructions as given with today's package of Certo.

Yield: six 8-ounce jelly jars

3½ cups cactus fruit juice
    (35-40 cactus fruit)
3½ cups sugar

Juice of 2 lemons
½ bottle Certo
(one 7-ounce pouch)

    "Pick half ripe cactus fruit with long handled meat fork to avoid spines. Place in pail and let water run into it to clean fruit. Put fruit in big pot, spines and all, and slice it in the pot. Add half a cup of water and cook until fruit is well done. Then put in a strainer and strain out juice, straining several times through double floursack cloth."

    To complete jelly-making process, follow instructions that come in each package of Certo. (Today's methods are simpler and more foolproof than those used in Mrs. Nimitz's time.). Pour into sterilized jars and let set.

Note: Cactus Fruit Jelly is commanding fancy prices in gourmet food shops in larger cities. The jelly has a beautiful deep-wine color and a distinctive flavor. However, the fruit is available only in late summer.

HOUSE SPECIALTIES

The name "Texas" is not of Spanish derivation as many people (even some Texans) believe but traces to the Hasinai Indians, a group affiliated with the Caddoans. Similar terms (tayshas, thecas, techan, teysas, techas, texias, tejas, texas) were used by the east Texas tribes, whose Hasinai greeted early Spanish explorers with "tejas," meaning friend. The explorers were soon referring to the area as the Land of the Tejas, or Texas. Its people subsequently took their names from the land, and Spaniards born there became Tejanos; Anglo-Americans of Colonial and Republic days were called Texians in English and Texiennes in French. Texican was an early variation. After statehood, Texas citizens were usually referred to as Texans, and the designation became official in 1860.

Texas Sweet Onion Relish

Use the mildest, sweetest onions available. Serve on toasted bite-size bread or crackers for an appetizer with special flavor and crunch.

Yield: 3 cups

3 large onions, thinly sliced and chopped
2 cups boiling water
1 cup sugar
½ cup cider vinegar
½ cup mayonnaise
Juice of ½ lemon
¼ teaspoon celery salt
¼ teaspoon Beau Monde Seasoning
¼ teaspoon paprika

Place chopped onions in a medium bowl. Combine water, sugar and vinegar in a small saucepan and bring to a boil. Pour over onions; cover and let stand, unrefrigerated, for 12 hours.

Drain and add mayonnaise, lemon juice and seasonings. Place in a jar and refrigerate. This will keep for 10-12 days.

Raspberry Sauce

Serve over ice cream, fresh peaches, hot waffles or use as a topping for your favorite cheesecake.

Yield: 1½ cups

1 10-ounce package frozen
  red raspberries, thawed
2 tablespoons currant jelly
1 tablespoon cornstarch
2 tablespoons orange juice

Drain juice from raspberries into a small saucepan, reserving berries. Add jelly to juice and heat until jelly is melted. Dissolve cornstarch in orange juice and add to mixture. Cook, stirring constantly, over medium heat until sauce becomes clear and thickens. Add raspberries and chill.

Fresh Mint and Currant Sauce

Mint is traditional with lamb because the flavors are so good together. You'll like this change from the usual mint jelly because of its fresh tangy taste.

Yield: 1 cup

⅓ cup minced fresh
  mint leaves
¼ cup white vinegar
2 tablespoons sugar
¾ cup water
1 tablespoon cornstarch
¼ cup currant jelly

Combine mint leaves, vinegar, sugar and water in a small saucepan. Stir cornstarch in a cup with small amount of mixture from the saucepan until dissolved. Pour into saucepan and heat until mixture becomes clear and begins to thicken. Add currant jelly and heat until dissolved. Refrigerate until ready to serve.

Some historians assert that Cabeza de Vaca, the first European visitor to what later became Texas, was shipwrecked at the mouth of Oyster Creek near Freeport. The fierce-looking Karankawa Indians inhabited the Gulf Coast at the time, camping along the creek and feasting on its fish and oysters. Nearby Chocolate Bayou—whose muddy waters bring hot chocolate to mind — really owes its name to a similar-sounding Indian word for the small, fiery chiltipiquin pepper that grows in the area.

Bea's Christmas Popcorn

A special treat to share with friends, neighbors and family during the holidays.

Yield: 5 quarts

5 quarts freshly popped, unsalted popcorn
1 cup unsalted, dry-roasted peanuts
1 cup butter or margarine
2 cups firmly packed light brown sugar
½ cup dark corn syrup
½ teaspoon baking soda
½ teaspoon vanilla

Combine popcorn and peanuts in a large, lightly greased roasting pan; mix well and set aside.

Melt butter or margarine in a medium saucepan; stir in sugar and corn syrup. Bring to a boil and continue boiling over medium heat for 5 minutes, stirring occasionally. Remove from heat, stir in soda and vanilla. Pour over popcorn mixture and stir until evenly coated.

Bake at 250° for 1 hour, stirring every 15 minutes. Remove from oven, cool for 10 minutes. Spread in single layer on folded large brown paper bags to cool completely. This will stay fresh tasting for 2-3 weeks if kept in an airtight container.

Toasted Croutons

Add a handful of these to your favorite tossed salad for more flavor and crunch. These are so much better than those you buy in a package.

Yield: 1 pint

6 slices bread (frozen slices
   will cut more evenly)
6 tablespoons corn margarine
½ teaspoon onion salt
½ teaspoon garlic salt
½ teaspoon dill weed

Remove crusts from bread and save for bread crumbs. Cut bread into ½-inch cubes and spread in a large, flat pan. Combine remaining ingredients in a small saucepan and heat until seasonings are dissolved. Pour over bread cubes, stirring to coat evenly. Bake at 225° for 1½-hours, stirring occasionally.

Dressing for Fruit Salad

Yield: 1 cup

1 3-ounce package softened
   cream cheese
2 tablespoons mayonnaise
6 tablespoons apricot
   preserves
1 tablespoon fresh lemon juice
¼ teaspoon curry powder
6 ounces whipping cream,
   whipped

Blend cream cheese with mayonnaise. Add preserves, lemon juice and curry powder (optional). Fold cheese mixture into whipped cream and chill. Serve on a fruit tray or toss with chunks of pineapple, oranges and kiwi fruit. This dressing will remain stable if stored in the refrigerator for a day or two.

Hot Spiced Cider

This drink is great for a crowd on a cool fall day.

Yield: 30 cups

1 gallon apple cider
32 whole allspice
32 whole cloves
4 cinnamon sticks
¼ teaspoon salt
1 cup brown sugar

Pour cider in a large kettle. Tie allspice and cloves in a cheesecloth bag and place in cider. Add remaining ingredients and simmer gently for 30 minutes.

Bloody Mary Special

Yield: 10 servings

18 ounces vodka
36 ounces tomato juice
⅛-¼ teaspoon salt
½ teaspoon black pepper
½ teaspoon celery salt
2 tablespoons Worcestershire sauce
1 tablespoon powdered sugar
Tabasco sauce to taste

Combine ingredients in a 2-quart container. Refrigerate overnight to allow flavors to blend. Serve garnished with thin slices of lime or long vegetable sticks.

Bob's Frozen Margaritas

Fill your glass with this frosty concoction and enjoy one of Mexico's greatest gifts to thirsty Texans.

Yield: 4 glasses

1 6-ounce can frozen concentrate for limeade
6 ounces tequila
3 ounces triple sec
½ tablespoon lime juice
10 ice cubes
Lime wedge
Salt

Combine limeade, tequila, triple sec, lime juice and ice cubes in a blender bowl. Blend for about 20 seconds or until ice cubes become slushy. At this point Margaritas may be stored in freezer. When ready to serve, rub lime wedge on rims of chilled glasses. Invert glasses on a generously salted surface so that salt adheres to the moistened rims.

Border Buttermilk

The Texans of the Rio Grande Valley consider this their special drink.

Yield: 4 servings

1 6-ounce can frozen lemonade concentrate (do not dilute)
1 lemonade can filled with tequila
Cracked ice

Place frozen lemonade and tequila in your blender bowl. Add cracked ice to fill bowl and blend until smooth.

Mama Perkin's Slang Jang

If you have a dish that needs a little zip, slang jang will do it. It's traditionally served over freshly cooked purple-hull or black-eyed peas or butter beans.

Yield: 3 cups

2 fresh tomatoes, finely chopped
½ medium bell pepper, finely chopped
½ medium onion, finely chopped
2-3 hot peppers, seeded and finely chopped
1-1½ cups cider vinegar
Salt and pepper to taste

Combine vegetables in a medium bowl. Add vinegar, salt and pepper and mix well. Refrigerate.

PBJR Spread (Peanut Butter-Jelly-Raisin)

When you need something that keeps without refrigerating, this can be a godsend. The raisins add nutrition and the jelly keeps the spread from being too dry. Needless to say, kids eat it up.

Yield: 2 cups

2 cups grape jelly
½ cup peanut butter
½ cup raisins

Combine in bowl of a food processor and process until raisins are finely chopped. Store in a jar. Refrigerate if spread is to be kept more than a day or two.

Microwave Hollandaise Sauce

A really easy way to make Hollandaise sauce that is quick and practically foolproof.

Yield: 1 cup

½ cup melted butter or margarine
1 tablespoon lemon juice
5-6 egg yolks
½ teaspoon salt

Microwave butter or margarine in a small bowl on Medium-High for 1 minute. Add remaining ingredients and beat until smooth. Microwave on Medium-High for 1 minute, stirring every 20 seconds.

Horseradish Sauce

Yield: 1 cup

½ cup mayonnaise
¾ cup sour cream
½ teaspoon dry mustard
1 teaspoon lemon juice
1 tablespoon prepared horseradish

Combine ingredients and serve with corned beef or ham.

Rosy Road Barbecue Sauce

Yield: 1 cup

½ cup catsup
½ cup orange marmalade

Combine and pour over grilled chicken for final 5 minutes of cooking, turning once. Tasty!

Auntie's Uncooked Chow-Chow

Yield: 4 pints

3 cups cider vinegar
2 cups sugar
1 teaspoon tumeric
1½ teaspoons prepared
  mustard
½ teaspoon celery seed
½ teaspoon mustard seed
½ teaspoon pickling spice
Juice of 2 lemons

Combine ingredients in an enamel or a stainless steel pan, bring to a boil and simmer for 5 minutes. Set aside to cool.

4 medium onions
8 cups chopped green
  tomatoes
½ stalk celery
½ small head of cabbage
1½ small hot peppers,
  seeded
3 sweet green or red
  peppers
½ cup pickling salt
  (or non-iodized)

Coarsely grind vegetables and mix together. Add salt and let stand for 20 minutes. Drain well; mix with cold vinegar solution. Spoon into sterilized jars and seal.

Hondo Pickled Beets

Yield: 4-6 pints

10 medium-size beets
   Water to cover
2 cups vinegar
2 cups brown sugar
½ teaspoon salt
½ teaspoon whole cloves
¼ teaspoon allspice
1 stick cinnamon

Wash beets, cover with water and cook until tender. Drain and cover with cold water. Remove skins and slice or cube. Combine remaining ingredients with beets in a large kettle. Simmer for 15 minutes. Spoon beets into sterilized jars. Cover with spiced vinegar and seal.

Gary's German Dill Pickles

These are wonderful dills that taste just like those Mom used to make.

Yield: 4 quarts

20-24 medium cucumbers
   8 large heads dill
   1 teaspoon alum
   4 cloves garlic
   9 cups water
   3 cups white vinegar
   ¾ cup pickling salt

Scrub cucumbers and pack into 4 sterilized quart jars. Place 2 large heads of dill and ¼ teaspoon alum in each jar. Slice garlic cloves in half and insert 2 pieces between cucumbers and sides of each jar. Bring water, vinegar and salt to a boil in a large saucepan and pour over cucumbers. Seal immediately.

House Specialties

Four months after the bones of 52 Texas patriots were interred at Monument Hill in La Grange in 1848, German immigrant Henry Kreische purchased 172 acres of the bluff property, including the tomb site. He constructed a house, barn, smokehouse, a large brewery (which ranked third in the state) and a dance pavilion on the land and became a prominent and popular La Grange citizen. Supposedly, a hoisted Frisch Auf! brewery flag signalled residents of the town below to come on up for German music and beer. Until his death in 1882, he conscientiously maintained the above-ground tomb and tried to protect it from vandals. When Julia, the last of his six unmarried children, died in 1952, the Catholic church received the property. It has been operated as the Kreische Brewery State Historic Site by the Texas Parks and Wildlife Department since 1977.

Cranberry-Orange Relish

A fresh-tasting relish that makes a special gift for friends during the holiday season.

Yield: 3 cups

3 cups cranberries (one 12-ounce package)
1 medium unpeeled orange (thin skinned)
¾ cup sugar
2-4 tablespoons orange liqueur

Wash berries, remove stems and drain. Wash orange well, remove stem end and cut into quarters. Remove seeds and excess white pith. Place berries and orange quarters in a food processor and pulse until finely chopped. Place orange-cranberry mixture in a large bowl. Add sugar, stir and set aside until sugar is dissolved. Mix in orange liqueur and refrigerate for at least 24 hours.

Tastes & Tales

INDEX OF RECIPES
INDEX OF TALES

Texas Lake Scene

Happy Cooking,

Y'all!

INDEX OF TALES

Special Thanks For Information Used In Tales:

Admiral Nimitz Museum,
    Fredericksburg, Carol Sattler
East Texas Oil Museum at Kilgore
    College, Kilgore
Fort Concho Museum, San Angelo,
    Robert Bluthardt
Sam Houston Memorial Museum,
    Huntsville
Scott & White Memorial Hospital,
    Temple, Don Nelson
Terlingua Foundation, Terlingua,
    Bill C. Ivey
Ysleta del Sur Pueblo Tigua
    Cultural Center, George Quinn

Contributors

Our very special thanks to the following great Texas cooks (and to a few transplanted Texans) who shared their recipes with us and made the writing of *More Tastes and Tales From Texas . . . With Love* a real pleasure.

Bobbie Adams . . . . Austin
Susie Bennett . . . . Dallas
Vera M. Boss . . . . Tyler
Velma Bowman . . . . Harlingen
Sue Braddock . . . . Leander
Karey Bresenhan . . . . Houston
Clarkie Mae Brown . . . . Lufkin
Elizabeth Bryant . . . . . Hot Springs, AR
J. Robt. Buckley . . . . Brownsville
Kandy & Dennis Burdette . . . Carrollton
Mabel Canfield . . . . George West
Carrabba's Italian Restaurant
. . . . Houston
Teddi Cherry . . . . Rowlett
Shirley G. Clement . . . . El Paso
Faye Clifton . . . . Lakeway
Aletha Cox . . . . Kilgore
Ada Crager . . . . Canyon
Dorothy Crockett . . . . . Horseshoe Bay
Teen Darden . . . . Clifton
Carolyn Davis . . . . Terlingua
Veda Dismuke . . . . Brownwood
Bea Dittrich . . . . Schulenburg
Beverly Dorsey . . . . Lakeway
Karen Eaker . . . . Uvalde
Delores East . . . . Galveston
Dottie Fields . . . . Lakeway
Mrs. R.S. Fillmore, Jr. . . . . Temple
Max Floerke . . . . Corpus Christi

Anita A. Fowler . . . . Pearland
Joan Herrmann Fox . . . . . Missouri City
Pat Frezzill . . . . Abilene
Lillian Fry . . . . Cisco
Martha Fuentes . . . . Brownsville
Donna Gaskill . . . . Wylie
Glenda Goodall . . . . Dallas
Leann Gordon . . . . Fort Worth
Toni Gosling . . . . Covington, LA
Bob & Betty Graham . . . . Austin
Doris D. Graham . . . . Midland
Betty W. Grainger . . . . Daingerfield
Cindy Grillo . . . . Sugar Land
Luisa Guzman . . . . Houston
Margaret Haegelin . . . . Hondo
Midge Hammock . . . . Clifton
Marvin G. Hein . . . . Lakeway
Sue Herbold . . . . Victoria
Ruby Hilburn . . . . Austin
Susan Granger Holcombe
. . . . Portsmouth, England
Gail Holden . . . . Georgetown
Virginia Hughes . . . . New Braunfels
D.W. Jacobson . . . . Comfort
Mrs. Lyndon B. Johnson . . . . Stonewall
Ramona Johnson . . . . Belton
Joyce Joiner . . . . Lakeway
Elizabeth Kaiser . . . . Fredericksburg
Elizabeth R. Kunze . . . . Victoria

Joanne Land . . . . Round Rock
Mrs. Curley Lange . . . . Port Neches
Catherine Lay . . . . Wellfleet, MA
Kathey Leewright . . . . Whitehouse
Julie Mabry . . . . Dallas
Mrs. Adele Maresh . . . . Caldwell
Fawn Mikel . . . . West Columbia
Jimmie Del Moore . . . . Athens
Mrs. Jack Mora . . . . Port Arthur
Evalene McDonald . . . . Plainview
Kathy McGough . . . . Nacogdoches
Wenonah I. Nagy . . . . Bryan
Shirley O'Connor . . . . Lakeway
Susanne Burns Payne . . . . Austin
Elouise L. Phelan . . . . El Paso
Mrs. Groner (J.B.) Pitts . . . Brownwood
Nancy Rector . . . . Kerrville
Elrose Renger . . . . San Antonio
Kay Rester . . . . Austin
Carol Sattler . . . . Doss
Nancy Jo Sick . . . . Houston
Sue Lowe Sims . . . . San Angelo
Jill H. Smith . . . . El Paso
Opal Smith . . . . China Spring
Sandra Smith . . . . Spring
Mary Rose Spann . . . . Pharr
Randy Speer . . . . Conroe
Mrs. W.E. Steele . . . . Alvin
Sandy Still . . . . Houston
Jan Temple . . . . Temple
Tigua Indian Reservation . . . . . . El Paso
Peg Tolzman . . . . Lakeway
Barbara Tompkins . . . . Midland
Beverly K. Tudor . . . . Port Neches

John Claus von Dohlen, Jr. . . . . . Goliad
Avis B. Voorhes . . . . Brownsville
Kay Walter . . . . Silsbee
Waterstreet Seafood Restaurant
. . . . Corpus Christi
Mrs. Ney Watson . . . . Hillsboro
Venna Mae Watson . . . . Lancaster
Bertha Weigler . . . . Austin
Adolph & Donna Wetegrove . . . Austin
Vicky Windham . . . . Austin
Wisialowski Family . . . . Houston
Ann Wuest . . . . Seguin
Betta Yeosock . . . . Fort Hood

Special Sources of Recipes:

Adam's Gift Shop, Round Rock
Air Terminal Services, Houston
C'Est Fini, Abilene
The Cooks Store, Galveston
Fredonia Hotel, Nacogdoches
Gruene Haus, Gruene
Kay's Hallmark, Austin
Leewright's, Tyler
M-Ruth's, Lancaster
Marine Military Academy,
    Harlingen
The Pan-Tree, San Angelo
Pauletta's Place, Austin
Scholz Garden, Austin
Texas Star, Spring
Totally Texas, Corpus Christi
Wenonah's, College Station
The Wooden Star, Houston
Y'All's Texas Store, Houston

Notes

Notes

Notes

To order additional copies of *Tastes and Tales From Texas . . . With Love,* or the second book entitled *More Tastes & Tales From Texas . . . With Love,* use the order blanks below.

Hein & Associates
5446 Highway 290 West
Austin, Texas 78735

Tastes & Tales

A Collection of Texas Recipes
By Peg Hein

Please send _____ copies of *Tastes & Tales From Texas . . . With Love* to:

Name _____

Address _____

City_____ State_____ Zip Code_____

Enclosed is $11.00 plus $2.25 for postage and handling. Texas residents add an additional 88¢ sales tax.

The second book of Texas recipes and tales titled *More Tastes & Tales From Texas . . . With Love* contains Texas recipes and tales that are completely different from those in *Tastes & Tales From Texas . . . With Love.* If you would like to order it, please use the order blank below.

Hein & Associates
5446 Highway 290 West
Austin, Texas 78735

Please send _____ copies of *More Tastes and Tales From Texas . . . With Love* to:

Name _____

Address _____

City_____ State_____ Zip Code_____

Enclosed is $11.00 plus $2.25 for postage and handling. Texas residents add an additional 88¢ sales tax.